The Quilter's Kitchen

by
Darlene Zimmerman and Joy Hoffman

EZ International
95 Mayhill Street
Saddle Brook, NJ 07662

Acknowledgements

We want to thank both of our families for being helpful and patient with us as we worked on this project together. Life hasn't always been easy!

Thanks go to:

Chuck Sabosik at EZ International for his help and encouragement.

Mimi and John at SPPS, Inc. for putting the book together and for their friendship and helpful advice.

Mike Keefe of Popular Front Studios for his photography.

Bernina of America for the loan of a sewing machine.

Hobbs Bonded Fibers and Fairfield Processing Corporation for their generosity in supplying batting.

Special thanks to Karla Schulz and Nancy VanderVoort for their machine quilting.

And all the others who helped along the way.

Published in the United States by EZ International, 95 Mayhill Street, Saddle Brook, NJ 07662.
Printed in Hong Kong.   10 9 8 7 6 5 4 3

ISBN: 1-881588-04-1

We dedicate this book to our mothers who taught us
the fine arts of both cooking and sewing.

Thanks Moms!

Preface

Welcome To The Kitchen.

The Quilter's Kitchen was designed to provide something for everyone from the microwave magician looking for quick, simple projects, to the culinary expert who revels in the idea of intricate, far more complex patterns. Look for the apple rating given for each pattern. One apple is for simple patterns, and the more challenging patterns may have up to three apples. Choose something appropriate for your skill level.

Quilting and cooking are to many in the quilt world equally necessary. Borrowing from this assumption, The Quilter's Kitchen is intended to make both quilting and cooking a little easier as well as far more enjoyable. The EZ tools, both Companion Angle™ and Easy Angle™, will soon fall into the "I don't know how I managed before them" category. Study the Tool Tutorial and easily learn how simple it is to cut triangles, half-square blocks, and trapezoids of virtually any size needed. Go on to the *Basic Ingredients* and watch seemingly complicated quilts dissolve into simple components.

A working knowledge of Companion Angle™ and Easy Angle™ allows the quilter to change triangle sizes with ease. The "recipes" are written in table form to allow you to personalize the color placement and quilt size. Kitchen Math is a handy table of sizes and numbers. Use it to rapidly determine yardages needed if adding or subtracting blocks, making it painless to have *your* quilt *your* way.

Also, look for our tried and true food recipes sprinkled throughout the book.

We hope you find both the quilts and the food in good taste.

Table of Contents

Utensils, Ingredients, and Stirring the Pot

Using Companion Angle™

Use Companion Angle™ to cut triangles with the long edge on the outside of a block, border, or quilt. Cut the triangles with the long edge on the straight of the grain to prevent distortion.

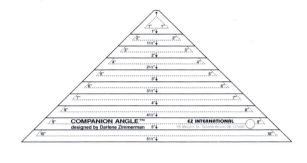

Dashed lines represent sewing lines and show the *finished* triangle size, based on a ¼" seam allowance; center numbers represent the width of the strip to cut; solid lines underneath are used for alignment (for example, cut a 2½" strip for *finished* 4" triangles.)

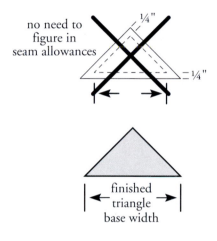

Determine the required size of the long edge of your finished triangle.

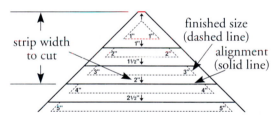

Determine the required strip width to cut to get the desired triangle size.

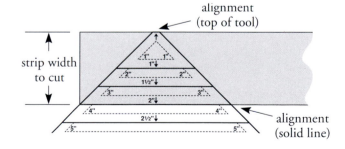

Align the tool edge with the edge of the strip.

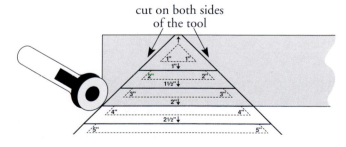

Cut on both sides of the tool.

9

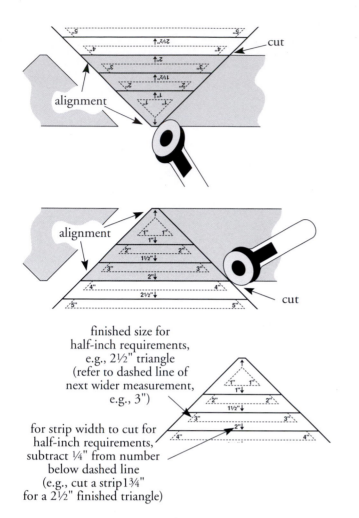

finished size for
half-inch requirements,
e.g., 2½" triangle
(refer to dashed line of
next wider measurement,
e.g., 3")

for strip width to cut for
half-inch requirements,
subtract ¼" from number
below dashed line
(e.g., cut a strip 1¾"
for a 2½" finished triangle)

Invert the tool and cut another triangle; continue in this manner across the strip of fabric.

As you continue across the strip, make sure that the top of the tool, the alignment line you are using, and the edge of the triangle are positioned correctly.

You can use this tool to cut triangles that have other than whole inch long edges. The role of the dashed and solid lines are reversed. Align on the dashed line.

Trapezoids

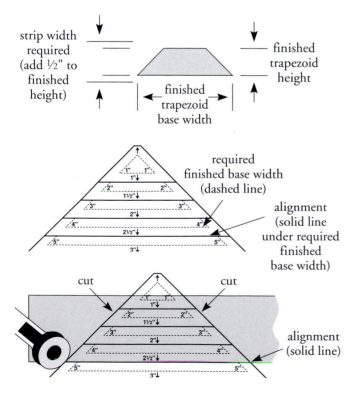

strip width
required
(add ½" to
finished
height)

finished
trapezoid
height

finished
trapezoid
base width

required
finished base width
(dashed line)

alignment
(solid line
under required
finished
base width)

cut   cut

alignment
(solid line)

To cut any trapezoid with Companion Angle™, you need to know the finished width of the base and the finished height. Add ½" to the height (two ¼" seam allowances) to get the strip width. Then use the tool just as you would for cutting triangles, using the base width as reference.

As an example, suppose a pattern calls for a trapezoid with a 4" finished base. Position your Companion Angle™ just as you would for a triangle with a 4" finished base. The only difference is the top of the tool will not align with the top of the strip.

Align the fabric strip to the alignment line so it extends on both sides of the tool. Cut on both sides of the tool. Then, just as you do when cutting triangles, flip the tool and cut the next one in the same manner.

Using Easy Angle™

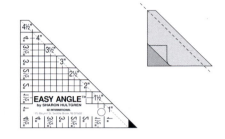

Easy Angle™ provides a quick method to cut right triangles. Just add seam allowance to your finished size, place two cut strips of fabric right sides together, then counter-cut with the Easy Angle™. The lines on the tool are provided at ¼" increments, and are used for aligning fabric strips for cutting. The heavier lines are provided at ½" increments.

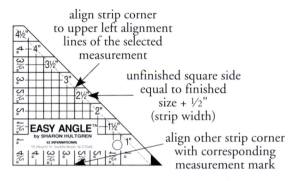

Use of the tool requires that you select a finished square size. Once you do this, add ½" to get the corresponding unfinished triangle size. Find the unfinished size on the tool and the alignment lines above and to the left of this number.

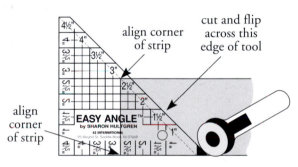

Cut strips equal to the unfinished width of the triangle size. Lay the strips right sides together. Align the bottom of the tool on the bottom edge of the strip. Slide the tool to the right until the end of the strip aligns with the strip width number at the bottom. Cut along the long edge of the tool.

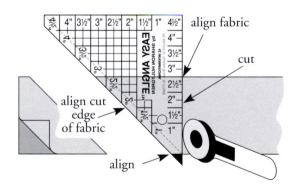

Flip the tool over the long edge and align the tool so that the cut edge of the fabric aligns with the tool and the bottom edge of the fabric aligns with the top of the black triangle on the tool. Cut along the perpendicular edge of the tool. Repeat these last two steps until you have cut all of your triangles. You will have pairs of triangles which you may string through your machine to make the triangle-squares. Note that the triangles are already right sides together.

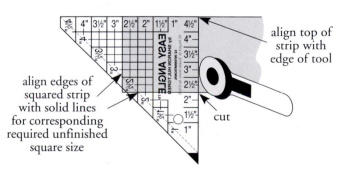

To make single fabric squares up to 4½", cut a strip equal to the unfinished square size. Align the tool with the top edge of the strip and slide it along the strip until the left side of the strip aligns with the vertical line on the tool representing the unfinished square size.

11

An Alternate Cutting Approach

Turn the Easy Angle™ so the little black triangle peak ("little mountain") extends past the *top* of the fabric strip and cut.

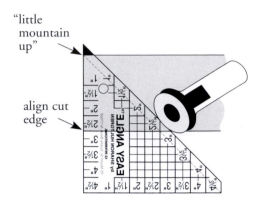

Turn Easy Angle™ 180° so the "little mountain" extends past the *bottom* of the fabric strip and cut.

Continue cutting in this sequence: "little mountain up; little moutain down". This method may work better for left-handed people.

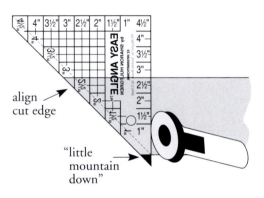

Triangle Tables

Use these tables to determine the number of Easy Angle™ or Companion Angle™ triangles you can expect to get from a 42" wide strip of fabric.

Easy Angle™		
Finished Size	Strip Width	Number
½"	1"	50
¾"	1¼"	42
1"	1½"	38
1¼"	1¾"	32
1½"	2"	30
1¾"	2¼"	28
2"	2½"	26
2¼"	2¾"	24
2½"	3"	22
2¾"	3¼"	20
3"	3½"	20
3¼"	3¾"	18
3½"	4"	18
4"	4½"	16

Companion Angle™		
Finished Size	Strip Width	Number
1"	1"	34
1½"	1¼"	27
2"	1½"	23
2½"	1¾"	20
3"	2"	17
3½"	2¼"	16
4"	2½"	13
4½"	2¾"	13
5"	3"	12
5½"	3¼"	10
6"	3½"	9
6½"	3¾"	9
7"	4"	8
7½"	4¼"	7
8"	4½"	7
8½"	4¾"	7
9"	5"	7
9½"	5¼"	5
10"	5½"	5

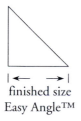

|← finished size →|
finished size
Easy Angle™

|← finished size →|
finished size
Companion Angle™

The above figures define the *finished* triangle sizes referenced in the tables.

Note: If the fabric width is more or less than 42", the number of triangles you may expect will be respectively more or less.

Half-Blocks

Quilt blocks set on point need half-blocks to complete the sides. These triangles should have the longest side cut on the straight grain of the fabric. Companion Angle™ can cut these half-blocks for your wall quilts – up to a 7" finished block. Use the table provided here to determine which size triangle to cut. Some of these triangles will be sightly larger than you need. That's okay! Trim carefully after sewing.

To cut the corner triangles, cut two squares the same size as your finished block, then cut on the diagonal. These will also be a bit larger than needed. Once again, trim carefully after sewing.

For larger half-blocks, measure the unfinished block, add two seam allowances and multiply this total by 1½. This should give adequately large half-blocks. Trim after sewing.

Half-block Cutting Directions		
Finished Block Size	Strip Width to Cut	Finished Triangle Size
2" block	2" strip	3" Companion Angle™ triangles
2½" block	2¼" strip	3½" Companion Angle™ triangles
3" block	2¾" strip	4½" Companion Angle™ triangles
3½" block	3" strip	5" Companion Angle™ triangles
4" block	3½" strip	6" Companion Angle™ triangles
4½" block	3¾" strip	6½" Companion Angle™ triangles
5" block	4" strip	7" Companion Angle™ triangles
5½" block	4½" strip	8" Companion Angle™ triangles
6" block	4¾" strip	8½" Companion Angle™ triangles
6½" block	5¼" strip	9½" Companion Angle™ triangles
7" block	5½" strip	10" Companion Angle™ triangles

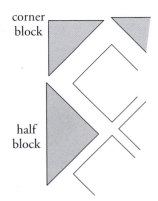

corner block

half block

for corner blocks use finished block size and cut diagonally

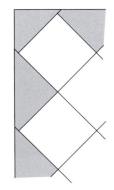

carefully trim after sewing (leave seam allowance)

for larger half blocks cut large square on both diagonals

Basic Ingredients

All the recipes in this "quiltbook" start with some very basic ingredients which are demonstrated in the following pages. These ingredients, just like the ones in your kitchen, can be combined in many ways to create everything from appetizers to desserts. There are directions for "doubling" the recipe given for many of the quilts to yield large quilts, as well as small projects perfect for the smaller appetite.

Remember when shopping for fabrics, choose high quality, 100% cotton. Vary the fabrics to create an interesting menu using prints of differing sizes and colors, from mild and mellow to bold and spicy. Use solids when intense flavors are needed and don't forget a little black. After all, when it's brown, it's cooking; when it's black, it's done!

Wash your fabrics before you start. Iron and straighten the grain if necessary. Cut carefully using an area with good lighting and then stitch accurate ¼" seams. This takes some practice, but stitching ¼" seams is a skill which is essential to quilt-making success. Consider investing in a special foot for your sewing machine for help in this area, or mark the ¼" allowance with masking tape on your sewing machine. Measure periodically to assure yourself that the ¼" seams being sewn are actually ¼". Rip out seams that need adjusting – break those eggs to achieve a really good omelet!

Triangle Squares

These handy little units are cut using Easy Angle™. The width of the fabric strip will be given in the recipe. Simply stack the strips right sides together and cut with Easy Angle™ (see *Tool Tutorial*). Chain stitch together.

Half-and-Half Units

Use Companion Angle™ to cut these shapes (see *Tool Tutorial*). The recipe will give strip width –

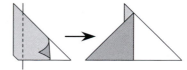

then stack strips right sides together, cut, then chain stitch together. Press towards the darker triangle. *Note:* It is important to have the correct fabric on top when stitching. Look for this direction in each recipe.

Broken Dishes Block

This block is simply two of the same Half and Half units stitched together. The seams will oppose naturally, making it easy to get a nice seam intersection in the center. Be careful – this block calls for a lot of bias edges to be stitched together – it can stretch easily so don't "toughen the dough" by handling it too much!

Flying Geese

Cutting instructions for this unit will include triangles cut with both Easy Angle™ and

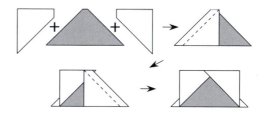

Companion Angle™ from fabric strips of the same width. The Companion Angle™ triangle makes up the "goose" and the Easy Angle™ triangles are the "sky". To assemble, stitch an Easy Angle™ triangle to the Companion Angle™ "goose" right sides together along the right side.

You can chain stitch lots of these units at the same time. Press towards the Easy Angle™ "sky". Add the second Easy Angle™ triangle to the left side forming the unit.

You may press this seam either to the "sky" or the "goose".

Note: When cutting Easy Angle™ triangles for flying geese,

some will be

and some will be

if your fabric has a right and wrong side. Simply divide these Easy Angle™ triangles into two groups. One group will be the right side of the flying goose, the other will be the left side. This allows you to line up the trimmed edges built into each tool.

Cream at the Top

This unit uses both Companion Angle™ and Easy Angle™ also. The Easy Angle™ triangles automatically have one "trimmed" corner. The opposite corner must also be trimmed for this block forming a special Easy Angle™ triangle. Do this

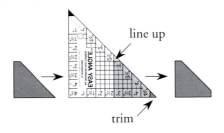

line up

trim

by simply turning the tool and trimming off the other "dog-ear".

Stack the special Easy Angle™ triangle right sides together with the Companion Angle™ triangle. The trimmed edges allow it to line up

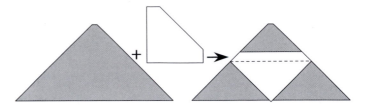

at only one place.

Stitch, trim the top of the Companion Angle™ triangle under the added Easy Angle™ triangle. Press seam towards the darker fabric.

Note: The top triangle may be light or dark, depending on your pattern.

Easy Angle™ / Companion Angle™ Orphans

At times recipes will call for single Easy Angle™ triangles or Companion Angle™ triangles. These triangles are stitched to various pieced units to complete the shape needed.

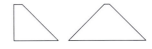

Quilt Jelly

Find a pretty jelly jar and place it in a handy place near your sewing table, ironing board, or cutting table. As you trim "dog-ears" from your quilt in progress, place the little bits in your jelly jar. When it is full, cover it with a small square of fabric, and tie on a ribbon. Label it "Quilt Jelly" and give it to a near and dear friend, or keep it on display and tell your non-quilting friends you save your "leftovers" to make miniatures.

General Quilting Information

In this section we will give general information on quilt-making. Please read through any sections on which you are unfamiliar, or which may have given you difficulty in the past. Our aim is to make the entire quilt-making process as enjoyable and as simple as possible. Also, read through each pattern before you begin. Although we don't say to do so in the directions, it is a good idea to make a sample block before you cut all the pieces needed for your quilt. You may wish to change or rearrange some of your fabrics. Also, you can catch any cutting errors before you've wasted lots of fabric.

Project Sizes

The projects in this book encompass a wide variety of sizes from tiny miniatures to large bed quilts. Many of the photographs are of quilts with dimensions appropriate for a throw or lap quilt. Consider that a quilt this size looks great on a sofa, folded on the foot of any size bed, as a wall-hanging for some of those big, blank walls (your stairwell maybe?) or as a child's "nappy" blanket. These quilts would make wonderful gifts for graduates or brides who would love a quilt as a gift. Is there a fabric that really catches your eye but doesn't "go" with anything in your house? A smaller quilt allows you to use this fabric, experiment and learn from your color choices, and have a quilt that is finished and ready to enjoy without worrying about carpet color, curtains, or where you will put it. A throw can simply be enjoyed and loved anywhere.

Many sizes have been included in cutting directions and fabric requirements but naturally everyone has a different size or purpose in mind. *Kitchen Math* was included to make the task of adding or subtracting blocks as simple as possible. Chose exactly the size you need; smaller to fit a bunk bed, or bigger for your son

who is 6'- 4" tall and growing. Using this size, determine the number of blocks you need to add or subtract. Count the number of triangles needed for that number of blocks and flip to *Kitchen Math*. These tables tell the number of strips needed for that number of triangles. Now multiply the number of strips by the strip width, and the fabric requirements magically appear, quickly and accurately. No more guessing about how much fabric you will need and ending up with two inches short or miles too long. The money you save by not making extra trips to buy more fabric and the time you save by not trying to figure out what to do with extra "leftovers" can be better spent on your next project.

Color and Fabric Selection

What makes a quilt a "show stopper" versus just O.K.? Pattern and workmanship play important roles, of course, but the fabrics selected are just as critical. Consider the following guidelines when choosing fabrics for a project.

Begin by choosing a fabric with character, an interesting design, colors that are dynamic, or something that catches the eye. Add fabrics to this beginning choice. The background fabric should be subtle but not boring. Consider a tone-on-tone or a tiny all-over print for this purpose. These prints are delicate and quiet, but add dimension and depth to the finished quilt.

Most patterns require a dark fabric to help define both design and colors. Black may be used for this purpose. If black seems too strong or not appropriate, consider any solid color that compliments the color scheme of the quilt. Solid fabrics are very intense and keep the other fabrics from melting into each other. Remember that fabrics with a design may read as solid colors from a distance and therefore are wonderful for this role.

The fabrics used need to be varied to provide interest. A quilt made totally of solid fabrics will make a dramatically strong statement. Too many lively prints mixed together may create chaos rather than interest. Learning how much spice to add is a skill that simply needs practice. If the color choices seem questionable, make one or two sample blocks, pin them to a wall and consider them from a distance. Rearrange the fabrics within the block; perhaps this may be a quilt that needs a dark background to show off a lovely light-colored print rather than the traditional light background with dark components.

Lastly, remember to please yourself. If the look you wanted was soft and muted for a baby quilt or to tone down some really wild wallpaper, delicate colors that blend gently will be exactly right. It's O.K. to break the rules and important to use the fabrics you like.

If you really don't like a fabric even after considering it in the context of the entire quilt; don't use it. That fabric will probably haunt you for the life of the quilt. Be open to suggestions and changes, but make the final decisions yourself.

Quarter Inch Seams

Sounds simple enough to sew a ¼" seam, doesn't it? Sewing a consistently *accurate* ¼" seam is crucial to quilt-making, and an important skill to master. To find that exact ¼" on *your* sewing machine, place one of your acrylic rulers under your presser foot. Lower the presser foot and line up the needle exactly on the first ¼" marking. Place masking tape on the machine snugly against the edge of your ruler. Use this as an accurate seam guide. Some sewing machines have a ¼" foot designed with quiltmakers in mind. It's worth investing in this special ¼" foot to make your piecing easier and more accurate.

Alternating Seams

Before sewing, wherever pieces must match up at a seam, line up the seams right sides together, having the seams alternating and pin at each intersection. As you sew the pieces together, it is also helpful to alternate the direction the seams are pressed. This will eliminate some of the bulk you get when several seam allowances come together.

alternate seam allowances
between pieces being
sewn together

As you come to each pin, remove it before sewing over the seam. You don't want your needle to hit one and break, flying off into oblivion!

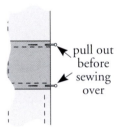

pull out
before
sewing
over

Chain Sewing

Another technique that should be used whenever possible is chain-sewing. Have the units stacked up next to your sewing machine and simply feed one unit after another through the machine without lifting the presser foot or cutting the thread. This saves time, thread, and helps to eliminate the "gobbling feed dog" problem. After chain-sewing them through, you will need to snip them apart before pressing.

Pressing / Stack pressing

Small arrows appear in several locations in this book showing pressing directions. If you follow these pressing directions, most, if not all of your seams will alternate. You certainly don't want seam allowances to stack up at an intersection. When pressing the pieces, use a dry iron. Steam is helpful in the final pressing of a quilt top.

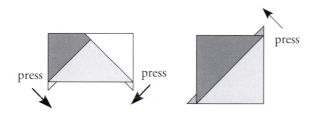

Stack Pressing

Stack pressing is a neat, efficient way to press small units such as triangle-squares or flying geese. This is especially helpful when your pieces are tiny. Simply place all units to be pressed by your left hand, dark side up. Lift the corner of the dark triangle, place it on the ironing board, and press the seam towards the dark triangle with the iron in your right hand. Now, pick up the next unit, lay it on top of the first unit pressed, lining up the raw edge of the

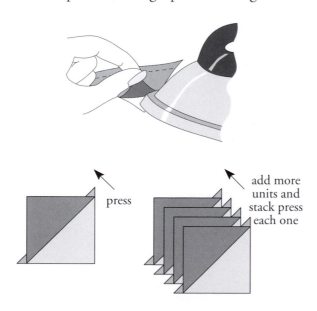

seam to the previous seam, and press again. Continue in this manner until the stack becomes too thick. (Reverse the procedure if you are left-handed.) This method is not only efficient, but prevents your units from being pressed out of shape.

To Rip or Not To Rip?

Ideally, if one cuts, pins, sews, and presses carefully, one should never have to rip! Unfortunately, none of us is perfect, and sometimes points do get cut off, or seams don't quite match up. Then the question arises – to rip or not to rip? There are several ways to look at this situation. First, it only takes a few minutes to take out and resew that mistake, whereas, if left, it will always be seen. You, however, are the quilter – you have to decide if you can live with the mistake or not. Everyone has a different tolerance level. Extra care in workmanship gives a sense of pride in accomplishment rather than a reason to apologize.

The Amish would put a deliberate mistake in their quilt because only God is perfect. Remember too, what we are creating is not a machine-made blanket, but a warm and loving piece of folk-art which does not have to be perfect.

For everyone out there who is wielding a seam ripper we have these words of advice:

1. Fix it if it bothers you.

2. Analyze the problem, don't just rip out and resew without solving the underlying problem.

3. Only rip something out three times. If you haven't fixed it by then, it isn't going to be fixed, and the fabric is suffering.

If Your Cake Falls...

We don't like to anticipate problems, but if you've ever had any of these difficulties before, read through the solutions and avoid any future problems.

Blocks the Wrong Size?

Check your seam allowances. You are probably sewing slightly more or less than a ¼". Even a tiny amount can add up to a big difference in a block. How to fix it? If all your blocks are approximately the same size, just cut your sashing and/or plain blocks to that measurement. Make lemonade out of your lemons!

Borders Ripple?

It is very important to measure and pin. Your border is probably bigger than your quilt. Re-read the sections on borders (page 21) – and yes, you should rip it out and fix it; those borders will never lie flat, even after quilting.

Oops! Out of Fabric?

Once again, look for ways to make lemonade out of your lemons. Don't be afraid to add another fabric. You could substitute another fabric in the same color family. It wouldn't have to match, it could be darker or lighter. Be creative! Arrange your blocks differently. Can some of the blocks be different? Your creative solution may make your quilt even better!

If Your Fabric Bleeds...

Hopefully, you will find this out when you're prewashing your fabric. (Yes, you must prewash your fabrics.) If it won't stop bleeding why take a chance? Substitute another fabric. If it's already in the finished quilt, try washing the entire quilt again, and then drying it as quickly as you can – yes, even in the dryer. It gives the fabric less time to bleed.

If Your Quilt Dies...

You thought it would be beautiful in those soft colors, but you laid out the blocks and it just died. The problem is you haven't chosen colors with enough contrast. Can you add sashing or an interesting border to revive it? A good rule of thumb to remember is to always use one dark color somewhere in your quilt. If color selection seems difficult for you, choose smaller projects that can be done in a number of color schemes as a learning experience. Discover what is pleasant to your eye and please yourself.

You Have a Closet Full of Quilt Tops...

Join the crowd... remember we're having fun! To get your quilts into use – machine quilt those tops or have someone do it for you. Join a quilt guild for inspiration and incentive. If you wish to hand-quilt, but the job looks overwhelming – just get started! You will be pleasantly surprised at how much can be accomplished in those spare minutes every day.

Finishing Your Quilt

Borders – Simple and Mitered

Almost every quilt has a border. Don't neglect this part of the quilt. Think of the border as a frame for your quilt. It is preferable to use the same colors in the borders which were used in the blocks. Generally, the darker fabrics look best in the border and/or binding.

Whether you put on simple borders, pieced borders or mitered borders, it's important to measure through the middle of your quilt in several places and take an average of these measurements. You may find the edges of the quilt have stretched somewhat through handling. The borders can help "square-up" your quilt. It is especially important on wall-hangings to have borders that are even and ripple-free.

Mitered Corners – Made Easy With Companion Angle™

1. Add borders to all four sides of your quilt, allowing several extra inches for the borders to extend beyond the edges of the quilt and overlapping each other. Stitch to within ¼" from the corner.

2. Fold the quilt on the diagonal, right sides together, matching raw edges, and having the borders extending outward.

3. Lay Companion Angle™ on your quilt with the longest edge on the diagonal fold and the side on the raw edges. You can mark your sewing line on the borders with a pencil, pin and sew the mitered seam. Check the right side before you trim off the excess fabric. Or…

    If you're comfortable with making mitered corners, you may wish to eliminate the marking and go on with Step 4.

4. Extend Companion Angle™ ¼" beyond the fold. Align fold line with 10" dashed line.

This will add a seam allowance to your borders. Cut along the edge of your tool.

5. Pin and sew the mitered corner.

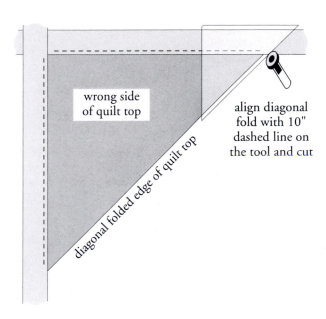

wrong side of quilt top

diagonal folded edge of quilt top

align diagonal fold with 10" dashed line on the tool and cut

Some of the quilts shown in this book have pieced or appliqued borders. Feel free to simplify these if you wish. Feel adventuresome? Add a pieced or appliqued border to add interest to your quilt.

Marking Your Quilt Top

It's a good idea to mark any quilting lines before you begin to baste your quilt together. There are many commercial quilting designs and stencils on the market, or be creative and design your own! The choice of marking pencils is varied – be sure to test any product on your fabrics first to see if it can be removed easily. Stitch-Thru™ Tear-Away Quilting Stencils are available to allow you to pin the quilting design on your quilt, then machine-stitch on the dotted lines, and tear the paper away. Isn't that easy?

Batting Choices

The quilt top is finished and ready for basting. The batting as well as the quilting should serve to enhance the top, transforming it into the finished quilt. Choose a batting to compliment the style of the quilt. A cotton batt that shrinks when washed will give an antique look that will be perfect for that 1930's style quilt. A fluffy polyester batt will be great for your toddler's "nappy" blanket that will need repeated washings.

For your wall-hangings you will wish to choose a flatter batt, either of cotton or polyester. Check your local quilt shop – many have samples of the various battings available to give you a better idea of the loft and texture of the different battings.

Basting Your Quilt Top

So now your top is finished and the quilting lines marked, but of course it's not a quilt until it's quilted. Whether you machine quilt or hand quilt, your quilt needs to be basted well for optimal results and to avoid those nasty ripples on the back.

Cut your batting and backing several inches larger all around than your top. Two inches would be the bare minimum, four inches is much better "insurance". Place your backing right side *down* on a flat surface and stretch it tight, either taping (with masking tape) or pinning it. Lay your batting on top, then your quilt top. Again, stretch and tape or pin the top. Now you are ready to pin or thread baste. Basting should evenly cover the surface of the quilt. Pins or basting lines should be no more than 4" apart.

Tip: A spoon (a grapefruit spoon) can help you to aim the point of the pin or needle back through the quilt layers.

Tip: If you wait to close the safety pins until after you've removed the tape securing the quilt layers, you'll find the pins easier to close.

Tip: Save those "trimmings" of batting from your projects to lengthen a batt or use in miniatures.

Hand Quilting

It's preferable to use hand quilting thread for quilting because of its durability and strength. Look for special quilting needles called "betweens". These are a short, strong needle. Use the smallest size you can thread and are comfortable with. A thimble will be very helpful in pushing the needle through the layers of the quilt. There are many types of thimbles available. Look for one you can be comfortable using.

The type of frame or hoop you choose is an entirely personal choice. You may even choose not to use one at all! If you don't use a frame or hoop, be certain your basting is adequate, and begin stitching in the center of your quilt.

There's no mystery to the actual quilting stitch – it's merely a running stitch catching all the layers of the quilt. Ideally your stitches should be straight, even and tiny. Don't despair – your quilting will improve with practice! All of your knots should be popped inside the layers and hidden.

Machine Quilting

Machine quilting requires a large working area for supporting the quilt while you're working on it. Set another table behind or beside your sewing machine. An extra pair of hands is also helpful. Now is the time to use your walking foot or even feed foot. This foot literally gives you two sets of feed dogs to help feed the top and bottom layers through the machine evenly. Do a test swatch with your fabrics and batting first; you may need to adjust your tension. When quilting long lines, alternate the direction the quilt is fed through. EZ International's Quilt Clips™ can help you to manage the bulkiness.

Use a good quality cotton-covered polyester thread or monofilament (invisible) thread (*not* hand-quilting thread!) for your top thread. Your bobbin thread can be either. Begin stitching, then after an inch or two, stop and pull your bobbin thread to the top. This will keep it from tangling in your sewing as you progress. Later, thread these tails on a sewing needle and bury the tails in the batting. This keeps the stitching from unraveling as the quilt is used and laundered.

A particularly useful and versatile method of quilting designs by machine is to use EZ International Stitch-Thru™ Tear-Away Stencils. Simply cut out the paper designs, center where you wish to quilt (you can see the quilt through the paper), pin to your quilt and machine stitch on the provided lines. Stitching is a continuous line. Stencils are available in a variety of sizes for open area quilting (e.g., plain blocks) and borders. Blank paper is available for creating your own designs. With Stitch-Thru™, there is no need to mark on your quilt top.

Free-Motion Quilting

Quilting designs having sharp curves may be smoothly quilted on the machine using a free-motion technique. This may be accomplished by dropping or disengaging the feed dogs (darning mode). Use a darning foot, a foot designed especially for machine quilting, or any foot that allows you a clear view of what you are sewing. Chew some gum, relax, and gently and evenly feed the quilt through the machine. Don't worry – you'll get better with practice!

Machine meandering or stippling can add an interesting effect to background areas, or can be used as an all-over quilting design. You do not need to mark the quilting lines on your quilt. Don't be intimidated by this – think of it as "doodling" with your sewing machine! Ideally the lines should be smooth, curved, and not cross each other. The meandering should resemble jigsaw puzzle pieces. Again, the more you do, the better the finished product becomes.

Combining Machine and Hand Quilting

Quilting in the 90's has combined both techniques for fabulous results. You may choose to machine quilt in the ditch and add beautiful hand-stitched accents, giving the look of an entirely hand-crafted quilt without as much time involved.

Bindings

After you've finished the quilting, it's time for the last step – binding. It's very important at this stage to take the time to either hand baste as close to the edge of the quilt as possible, or to pin and then machine-baste with the walking or even feed foot on your machine. This will prevent those three layers from shifting as you sew on the binding. *This step is very important; don't skip it!* Leave all the excess batting and backing on until *after* you've sewn on the binding. Then, when you're ready to turn back the binding, trim, allowing as much excess as you need to "fill out" the binding.

Straight-of-Grain Bindings

For miniatures and small wall-hangings we generally use a single, straight-of-grain binding. Double-fold binding may be too bulky for a small quilt needing binding that is narrow – just enough to stop the eye and finish the quilt edge. Straight-of-grain binding is fine for miniatures or small wall-hangings as the edge will not get a lot of hard use.

A double straight-of-grain or a double bias binding may be more suitable for a a larger wall hanging. A double binding will give a heavier and/or wider binding, more suitable for the larger block size. We recommend the double bias binding for bed quilts because of its added durability.

A general rule of thumb is to cut your binding four times the finished width (plus a little extra allowance for the bulk) for single fold binding, and six times the finished width for double binding. A finished ¼" single fold binding would begin as a 1¼" strip. A double binding would start with a 2½" wide strip, either bias or straight-of-grain, and finish to ½". For double binding, piece your strips as needed, then fold and press *wrong* sides together.

Whether using a single or double binding, start with a 45° angle cut

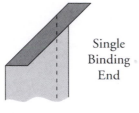

Single Binding End

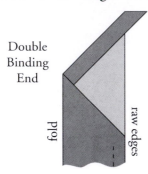

Double Binding End

fold

raw edges

with Companion Angle™. Turn the raw edge in ¼". Begin stitching 2" in from the beginning of your binding (this will make it easier to join at the end). Start at the lower right hand corner of your quilt. If using a double binding, have the raw edges of the binding aligned with the raw edges of your quilt. Stitch a ¼" seam until you get to exactly ¼" from the first corner. Stop

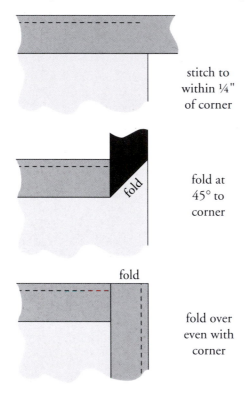

stitch to within ¼" of corner

fold at 45° to corner

fold over even with corner

and backstitch. (Your ¼" foot helps here!) Turn the quilt and the binding as shown in the diagram. Begin stitching at the edge until you get to the next corner. Repeat the procedure. To end the binding, simply overlap the two ends of the binding when using a single binding. (See diagram.) With a double binding, trim the end

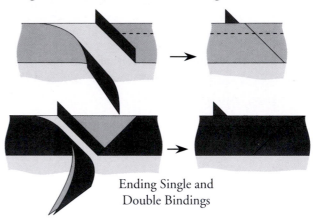

Ending Single and Double Bindings

at a 45° angle, and insert it inside the beginning of the binding. Finish stitching the binding down.

After the binding is sewn on and the excess batting and backing is trimmed away, turn the binding to the back side and blindstitch in place over the seam. Use thread that matches the binding and a fine thin needle (an applique needle works great). Don't allow your stitches to go through to the front of the quilt.

Sign and Date Your Quilt

Sign and date your masterpiece on the front if you like, or on the back side. You may wish to design a special label using either machine-stitched letters, or hand embroidered or cross-stitched letters. You could also sign and date your quilt with permanent pen and ink.

The
Quilt
Recipes

Chex Mix® / Jelly Beans 🍎🍎

10" x 11½"

See photographs on page 35.

Start the party off with these great nibblers. Chex Mix® and Jelly Beans both begin with the same basic recipe – a quick and simple block called "Broken Dishes". Give each miniature a different flavor by varying the fabric choices from mellow toasted tones to a true "party print".

Ingredients [1]		
Fabric #1		⅛ yard dark print
Fabric #2		⅛ yard light print
Fabric #3		⅛ yard medium print
Fabric #4		⅛ yard black

[1] Scraps or yardage

Cutting Directions		
From	Cut	To Get
Fabric #1	2 1" strips 1 2" strip	40 Companion Angle™ triangles [1] Outside border
Fabric #2	2 1" strips	40 Companion Angle™ triangles [1]
Fabric #3	1 1½" strip 1 1¼" strip	12 squares 4 Easy Angle™ triangles (corners) 14 Companion Angle™ triangles (edges)
Fabric #4	1 ¾" strip 2 1¼" strips	Inside border Binding

[1] Stack right sides together and cut with Companion Angle™. They will then be ready to chain sew.

The fabrics in the Ingredients Table are for Chex Mix®. Jelly Beans uses the same pieces, but use any color scheme you like. Three fabrics are used together in both borders and blocks for Chex Mix®. The orderly arrangement invites a second taste as the eye sees squares or is it stars? No, the Chex Mix® didn't burn; that little touch of black adds a delightful accent.

A vivid print is the main ingredient in Jelly Beans. Pair your "party print" with as many colors as you like. Mix thoroughly, garnish with an accent color, add that splashy border, and you have a miniature sure-to-please!

Quilt Assembly

Assemble 40 Half and Half units, having fabric #1 on the top. (See *Basic Ingredients,* page 15) Chain-sew them and press the seams toward the darker fabric (fabric #1) as indicated on the following page.

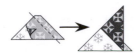

From your Half and Half units, assemble 20 Broken Dishes blocks. (See *Basic Ingredients,* page 15.)

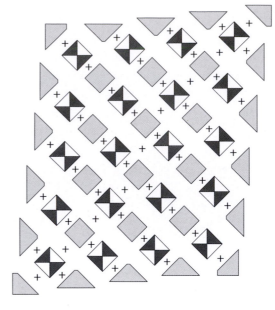

Assemble quilt in diagonal rows with alternating medium squares and Broken Dishes blocks, according to diagram above right. Press towards the medium squares and triangles. Note that the Broken Dishes blocks are turned a quarter turn in alternating diagonal rows.

Trim carefully, leaving a ¼" seam allowance as indicated in the diagram below right.

Add the tiny black border – be careful – don't burn the Chex Mix®!

Add the final border. (You may wish to add mitered borders instead of simple borders.)

Quilt, then bind in staight-of-grain binding and enjoy.

trim to ¼" from points

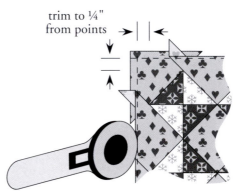

Party Mix

2	cups rice cereal	2	cups pretzels
4	cups Chex® cereal	2	cups nuts
1	cup butter	1½	cups sugar
½	cup white corn syrup		

Mix dry ingredients. Boil butter, sugar, and corn syrup for 4 minutes. Mix with dry ingredients and spread mixture on a cookie sheet until cool. Break apart and store in an airtight container.

Recipe by Karla Schulz

Raspberry Twirl / Black Cherry Delight 🍓

8¾" x 10¾"

See photograph on page 36.

Don't those luscious medium and dark purples make your mouth water? These fabrics may be a bit too much in large amounts, but they're perfect for miniatures. Look at the interesting effects you can achieve just by color placement.

Ingredients [1]		
Fabric #1		¼ yard dark
Fabric #2		¼ yard medium
Fabric #3		¼ yard light

[1] Scraps or yardage

Cutting Directions		
From	Cut	To Get
Fabric #1	1 1¼" strips	Binding
Fabric #1 or #2 [1]	2 1½" strips	48 Easy Angle™ triangles
Fabric #2 or #1 [1]	2 1" strips 1 1½" strips	48 Companion Angle™ triangles [2] Border
Fabric #3	2 1" strips	48 Companion Angle™ triangles [2]

[1] The dark and medium fabrics are interchangeable for the blocks , depending on the effect you desire to achieve.

[2] Layer fabric #3 and either fabric #2 or #1 right sides together; cut with Companion Angle™. They will then be ready to chain sew.

See photograph on page 36.

Quilt Assembly

Sew all the small triangles together into Half and Half units with the seam on the right and the darkest fabric on top. Press seam towards the darkest fabric.

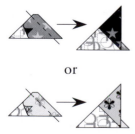

or

Add the large triangles. Press towards the largest triangle.

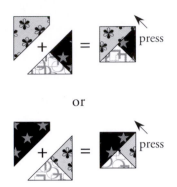

Join two units, giving the second unit a quarter turn. Make 24 of these units. Press to one side.

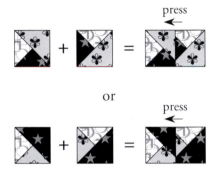

Reverse half of the rectangles. Join rectangles to form the pinwheel block. Press seams *open* to distribute seam allowances.

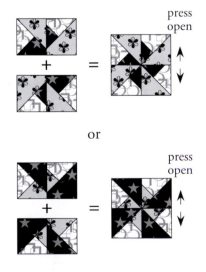

Join into rows, 3 blocks x 4 blocks.

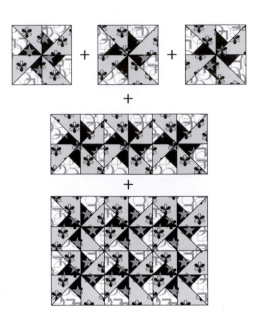

Add borders of either fabric #1 or fabric #2 cut at 1½".

Quilt an "X" in the ditch in each pinwheel block.

Bind in straight-of-grain single binding cut at 1¼", in the same fabric as the border.

Licorice Whips 🍅🍅

13" Square

Combine red and black to create a taste loved by kids of all ages. This quilt is not too tiny, yet small enough to be cute. Give it a try – who doesn't love a little licorice?

Ingredients		
Fabric #1		¼ yard
Fabric #2		¼ yard [1]
Fabric #3		¼ yard

[1] Includes straight-of-grain binding

See photograph on page 35.

Cutting Directions		
From	Cut	To Get
Fabric #1	1 1¼" strip 2 2" strips	20 Companion Angle™ triangles [1] Outside border
Fabric #2	1 1⅝" strip 1 1" strip	20 Companion Angle™ triangles [2] Inside border
Fabric #3	2 1¼" strips 1 3" strip	20 Companion Angle™ triangles [1] 20 Easy Angle™ triangles 4 Companion Angle™ triangles 4 Easy Angle™ triangles

[1] Layer fabrics #1 and #3 right sides together; cut with Companion Angle™. They will then be ready to chain sew.

[2] There is no line marked on Companion Angle™ for this size strip. Just line up the top of the tool and keep the bottom edge of the strip level with the other markings on the tool.

Quilt Assembly

Refer to *Basic Ingredients*, page 15, and assemble 20 Cream at the Top units from fabric #2

Companion Angle™ triangles, and fabric #3 Easy Angle™ triangles.

Appetizers

Assemble 20 Half and Half units from fabrics #1 and #3, with the fabric #1 triangle on top.

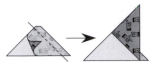

Sew these units to the Cream at the Top units to form 20 squares. Press towards the Cream at the Top unit. Stitch these together to form 5 Licorice Whip blocks.

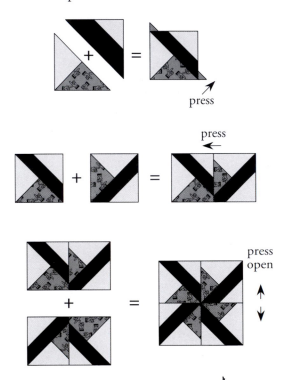

press

press

press open

Assemble quilt top according to the diagram in the next column, adding the Companion Angle™ and Easy Angle™ triangles on the sides and corners where shown. Press as indicated by the arrows in the diagram.

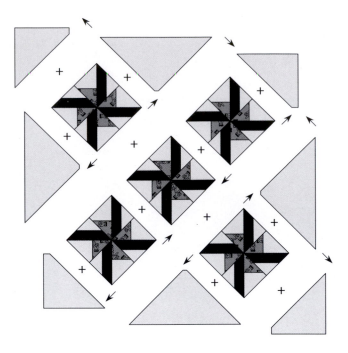

Trim square *carefully*, allowing ¼" seam allowance.

trim to ¼" from points

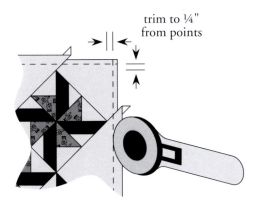

Add simple borders of fabric #2 and #1. (See *Finishing Your Quilt*, page 21, for instruction.)

Quilt each block in the ditch as indicated, and quilt as desired in open area.

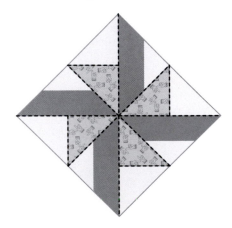

Caramel Fruit Dip

Recipe by
Joy Hoffman

| 8 | oz. cream cheese | ½ | cup caramel ice cream topping |
| ½ | cup crunchy peanut butter | | |

Soften cream cheese. Stir in peanut butter and add ice cream topping to taste. Serve with assorted fruit on skewers.

Sally's Popcorn Treat

14	cups popped popcorn	1½	lbs. white almond bark
3	cups Rice Krispies™	3	tbsp. peanut butter
2	cups peanuts		

Mix popcorn, Rice Krispies™, and peanuts. Melt together white almond bark and peanut butter. Toss together. Cool and enjoy!

Recipe by
Joy Hoffman

Cheese Bread

Recipe by
Karla Schulz

| 1 | pkg. shredded Mozzarella cheese | ½ | cup mayonnaise |
| 1 | stick margarine | ½ | pkg. ranch dressing (dry) |

Soften margarine. Mix ingredients and spread on a loaf of French bread that has been split in half. Bake at 375° until cheese is melted and bubbly.

Swedish Nuts

2	egg whites	⅔	cup butter
1	pinch of salt	3½	cups walnuts
1	cup sugar		

Beat egg whites until foamy. Add sugar and beat until firm, but not dry. Melt butter on cookie sheet. Mix walnuts with meringue. When coated with meringue, fold in butter, mixing as much as possible. Bake at 325°, stirring every 10 minutes, until butter is incorporated and nuts are golden brown.

Recipe by
Maureen Ohland

Artichoke Dip

1	large can unmarinated artichoke hearts	1	cup mayonnaise
1	cup Parmesan cheese	½	cup Mozzarella cheese
		1	pinch garlic salt

Blend ingredients with mixer until smooth (approximately 1½ minutes). The artichokes won't be completely mixed. Bake uncovered at 350° for 25-30 minutes. Serve hot with crackers or cucumber slices or spears.

Recipe by
Maureen Ohland

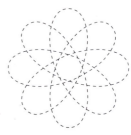

BLT Squares

1	8 oz. can refrigerated crescent rolls	6	bacon slices
1	8 oz. pkg cream cheese	¼	cup chopped green onion
1	chopped tomato		shredded lettuce

Fry or microwave bacon until slices are crisp. Crumble bacon. Press crescent roll perforations together to form a single sheet on a 9" x 13" baking sheet. Bake at 375° for 10-15 minutes. Cool. Combine cream cheese, green onion, and bacon bits. Spread over crust. Top with chopped tomatoes and lettuce. Cut into small squares and serve.

Recipe by
Joy Hoffman

Marinated Tomatoes

1	clove garlic, minced	¼	cup vinegar
1	tsp. thyme	⅓	cup oil
¼	cup sliced green onions	¼	cup parsley
1	tsp. salt	¼	tsp. pepper
1	pint cherry tomatoes, halved		

Place cherry tomatoes in a shallow pan. Combine marinade ingredients in a covered jar. Shake well. Pour over tomatoes and chill for two hours. Serve with toothpicks or tiny forks.

Recipe by
Joy Hoffman

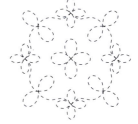

Caramel Corn

8	qts. popped popcorn	½	cup corn syrup
2	cups brown sugar	1	tsp. vanilla
1	cup butter	½	tsp. baking soda

Combine brown sugar, butter, and corn syrup in a saucepan. Boil gently for 5 minutes. Add baking soda and vanilla. Toss with popped corn. Place in a large roaster and bake for 1 hour at 250°.

Recipe by
Joy Hoffman

Jelly Beans
10" x 11½"
(See page 27)

Chex Mix®
10" x 11½"
(See page 27)

Licorice Whips
13" x 13"
(See page 31)

Raspberry Twirl
Black Cherry Delight
8¾" x 10¾"
(See page 29)

Afternoon Tea
37½" x 37½"
(See page 47)

Apple Cider
10¼" x 13"
(See page 52)

Mint Julep
38" x 51"
(See page 50)

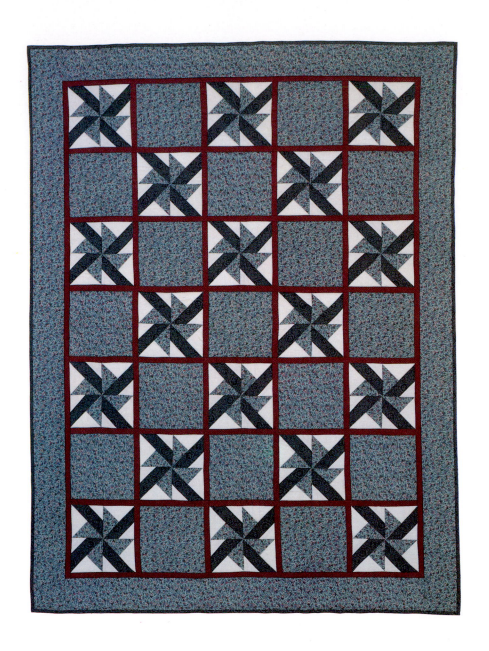

Mint Julep
38" x 51"
(See page 50)

Jello Salad
17" x 17"
(See page 56)

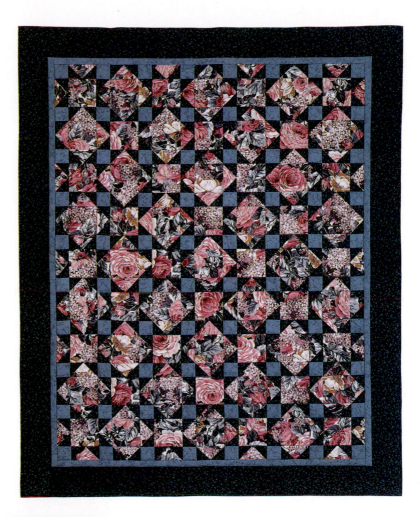

Garden Salad
54" x 66"
(See page 58)

Three Bean & Button Salad
50" x 62"
(See page 60)

Porcupines
63½" x 88"
(See page 64)

Pink Porcupines
71½" x 95½"
(See page 66)

Christmas Goose
30" x 30"
(See page 67)

Christmas Gosling
10" x 10"
(See page 69)

California Hotdish
47½" x 60"
(See page 70)

Beef Burgundy
60" x 80"
(See page 72)

Bread Pudding
42" x 56"
(See page 76)

Blueberry Freeze
60" x 74"
(See page 78)

Black Forest Torte
28" x 38"
(See page 79)

Caramel Apples
41" x 41"
(See page 82)

Ginger Star
18" x 18"
(See page 84)

Garnishes
(See page 88)

Afternoon Tea ❀❀❀

37½" Square (7½" Blocks)

See photograph
on page 36.

Those lovely Victorian prints with their luscious colors of plum, raspberry and rich deep greens bring to mind an elegant English tea, complete with delicate china, special teas, and dainty cakes. Our version of Afternoon Tea uses these lovely Victorian prints and colors and a "Cakestands" block set on point in a wall quilt to bring an elegant touch into your home.

Ingredients		
Fabric #1		⅔ yard background
Fabric #2		1½ yard large floral
Fabric #3		¼ yard light pink
Fabric #4		⅓ yard plum
Fabric #5		⅔ yard dark green [1]

[1] Includes double straight-of-grain binding

Cutting Directions		
From	**Cut**	**To Get**
Fabric #1	3 2" strips	10 - 5" x 2" rectangles
		5 - 2" squares
		10 Easy Angle™ triangles
		10 Companion Angle™ triangles
	1 3½" strip	5 Easy Angle™ triangles
	4 2¼" strips	56 Companion Angle™ triangles [1]
		16 Easy Angle™ triangles [1]
Fabric #2	1 4¾" strip	5 Companion Angle™ triangles
	1 2" strip	10 Easy Angle™ triangles
	1 12¾" square	4 half block triangles [2]
	2 7½" squares	4 corner triangles [2]
	2 1¾" strips	16 - four-patches [1]
	4 2½" strips	Fourth border
Fabric #3	1 3½" strip	5 Easy Angle™ triangles
	2 1¾" strips	16 - four-patches [1]
Fabric #4	1 2" strip	20 Easy Angle™ triangles
	2 3" strips	16 - 3" squares [1]
Fabric #5	12 1" strips	Sashing around blocks
		Inside border
		Third border

[1] For pieced border.
[2] See page 14.

Add small basket triangles to background rectangles, 5 one way, and 5 the other way. Press towards small triangles.

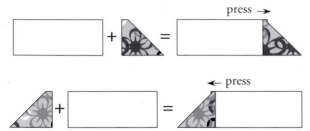

Add rectangles and bottom background triangle to large basket triangles. Press as indicated.

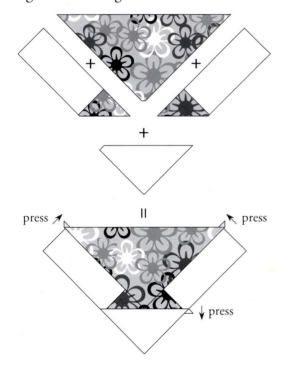

Assemble 10 pairs of triangle squares, pressing towards the darkest fabric.

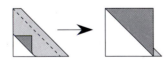

Assemble 5 units:

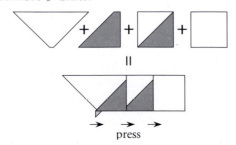

Assemble 5 units:

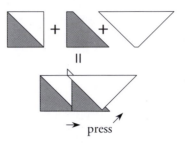

Add these completed units to the basket center. Press towards the center.

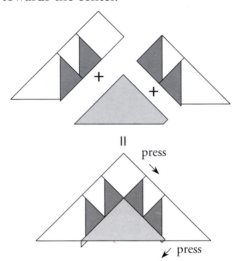

Complete the blocks.

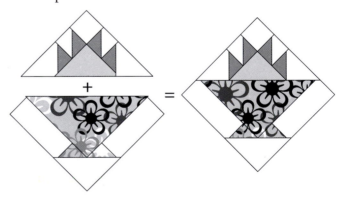

Add sashing strips as shown on the next page. Sew three blocks together with sashing between them, then add sashing strips to the two long sides of this row. Sew half blocks to both sides of the other two blocks, then sew these to the sides of the center row. Press towards the sashing. Add corner triangles last. See page 14 for cutting corner and half blocks.

Trim the quilt top square, *leaving ¼" seam allowance all the way around.*

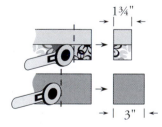

trim to ¼"
from points

Add a 1" border of fabric #5 around the quilt, or whatever size you need to make the quilt measure 25¼" square, which includes seam allowance. (*This is important if your next border is to fit properly.*)

Pieced Border

Sew right sides together the two 1¾" wide strips from fabrics #2 and #3. Press seam to one side. Cut these long strips into 32 - 1¾" pieces. You will also cut 16 - 3" squares from the 3" strips of fabric #4.

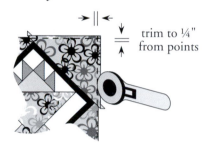

1¾"

3"

Sew the fabric #2 and #3 pieces together in pairs of two, alternating colors to make 16 four-patches as indicated.

Assemble border, adding background triangles as indicated between squares set on point. Begin with a checkerboard square on the short sides (4 checkerboard and 3 solid squares), and begin

with a solid square on the long sides (5 solid and 4 checkerboard squares). Notice you use the Easy Angle™ triangles at the beginning and end of each border, and the Companion Angle™ triangles in between. (*Tip: If you cut the tips off the Companion Angle™ triangles with your Easy Angle™, you will find them much easier to sew to the squares.*)

Finish with another 1" border of fabric #5, and a 2½" border of fabric #2.

The quilt was quilted very traditionally by hand ¼" from the seam lines. 1½" cross-hatching was done in the large portion of the basket and in the half blocks. A simple design was quilted in the last border.

Bind in double or single straight-of-grain binding with fabric #5.

Mint Julep 🍎

38" x 51" (6" Block)

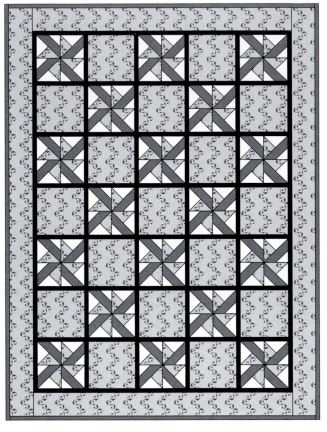

Choose shades of green ranging from mint to teal, garnish with a bit of candied violet and you have a lap quilt that looks as cool and refreshing as its name. For a larger quilt make the quilt we've named "Beef Burgundy" (page 72), which uses a larger block in a different setting. Want just a sip? Try "Licorice Whips" – it's a tiny "Mint Julep" block set on point without sashing (page 31).

Ingredients		
Fabric #1		½ yard background
Fabric #2		1½ yards print
Fabric #3		1 yard accent [1]
Fabric #4		½ yard sashing

[1] Includes ½ yard for double straight-of-grain binding

See photographs on pages 37 and 38.

Cutting Directions		
From	Cut	To Get
Fabric #1	7 2" strips	72 Companion Angle™ triangles [1] 72 Easy Angle™ triangles
Fabric #2	5 2" strips 3 6½" strips 5 3½" strips	72 Companion Angle™ triangles [1] 17 squares for plain blocks Outside borders
Fabric #3	6 2⅝" strips	72 Companion Angle™ triangles [2]
Fabric #4	11 1" strips 5 1" strips	28 - 1" x 6½" sashing strips 6 horizontal sashing strips Inside border

[1] Layer fabrics right sides together and cut Companion Angle™ triangles. They will then be ready to chain-sew.

[2] There is no marking on Companion Angle™ for this size. Just line up the top edge of the fabric with the top of the tool and keep the bottom of the fabric parallel with tool lines.

Quilt Assembly

From the 72 Companion Angle™ triangles you cut from fabrics #1 and #2, make 72 Half and Half units. (See *Basic Ingredients,* page 15.) Sew with fabric #2 on top. Press towards the darkest fabric.

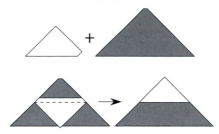

From the fabric #3 Companion Angle™ triangles and the fabric #1 Easy Angle™ triangles, make 72 Cream at the Top blocks. (See *Basic Ingredients,* page 15.)

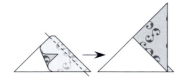

Join the Cream at the Top units to the Half and Half units to form part of the Mint Julep block. Press seam towards the Cream at the Top unit. Make 72 of these combined units.

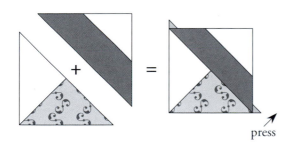

Join 4 of these units as shown to make the Mint Julep block. Make 18 Mint Julep blocks.

Alternate Mint Julep blocks with plain blocks, placing sashing between each block and

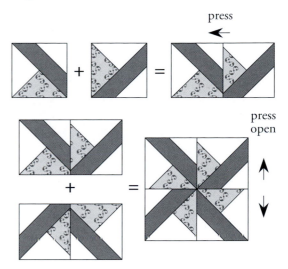

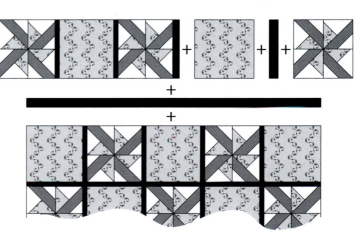

between rows. Join rows, alternating Mint Julep blocks. *Be sure to exactly match up the vertical sashing rows.* Press seams towards the sashing.

Add an inside simple border of fabric #4, and an outside border of fabric # 2.

Quilt as desired. We used EZ International Stitch-Thru™ pattern #6102 in the border. Bind in double straight-of-grain binding with fabric #3.

Apple Cider 🍎🍎

10¼" x 13"

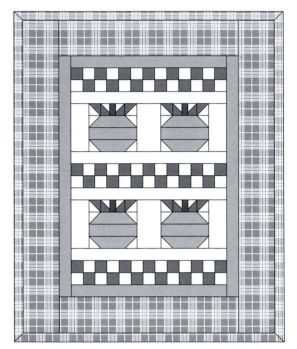

See photograph on page 37.

There's nothing like a hot mulled apple cider on a cold winter day. This little quilt can give you that same warm-to-the-toes feeling just by looking at it.

Cutting Directions

From	Cut		To Get
Fabric #1	2	1" strips	8 - 2" trapezoids [1] 4 - 1" x 2½" rectangles Inside border
Fabric #2	2	1" strips	16 Easy Angle™ triangles [2] Checkerboard strips
Fabric #3	3	1" strips	32 Easy Angle™ triangles [2] 4 - 1" x 7" strips [3] Checkerboard strips
	1	1½" strip	6 - 2½" x 1½" strips
Fabric #4	1	1" strip	4 - 1" squares for stems
Fabric #5	1	2" strip	Outside border

[1] Align trapezoid base on the solid line below the Companion Angle™ 2" dashed line, as if cutting a 2" finished size triangle. See page 10.

[2] Lay fabric #2 and #3 strips right sides together and cut 16 Easy Angle™ triangle squares for your leaves. You will also need to cut 16 Easy Angle™ orphans from fabric #3.

[3] Cut the size needed to match the length of your checkerboard strips.

Ingredients

Fabric #1		Red scraps
Fabric #2		Green scraps
Fabric #3		Background scraps
Fabric #4		Brown scraps
Fabric #5		Plaid scraps

Quilt Assembly

Add the Easy Angle™ orphans from fabric #3 to your fabric #1 trapezoids. Press towards the trapezoids.

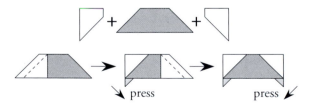

Assemble all your fabric #2 and #3 triangle squares. Press and trim "dog-ears". Join two triangle squares in each of the two ways shown here to form opposing leaves for each apple.

You will need to sew 4 of these sets of leaves.

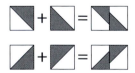

Fold the 1" stem square in half, right sides out, and insert in the seam between the two leaves (leaves will be right sides together with the folded square sandwiched between them.) Stitch and press the seam open on the back side. At the same time, open the stem and press it flat,

centering it over the seam. It will be loose (three dimensional), and that's great!

Add leaf strips to trapezoid strips and center apple strip to form the apples. Press the seams

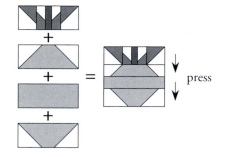

towards the bottom of the apples. Make four apples.

Assemble two sets each of two apples and three fabric #3 strips in the sequence as shown.

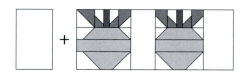

Sew 1" strips of fabric #2 and #3 together. Press towards fabric #2. Cut apart into 1" strips. Reassemble into checkerboard strip. You should have 13 units in each checkerboard strip. Press all the seams in one direction.

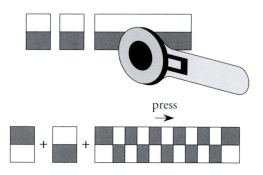

press →

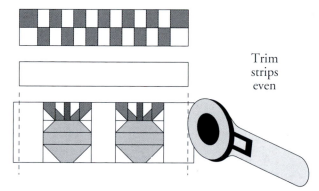

Trim your spacing strips and your apple strips to match the length of the checkerboard strips.

Trim strips even

Assemble three checkerboard strips, four 1" x 7" background strips, and two apple strips as indicated in the completed figure.

Add your inside border of fabric #1 and outside border of fabric #5.

Quilt as desired. Bind in single straight-of-grain binding in fabric #5.

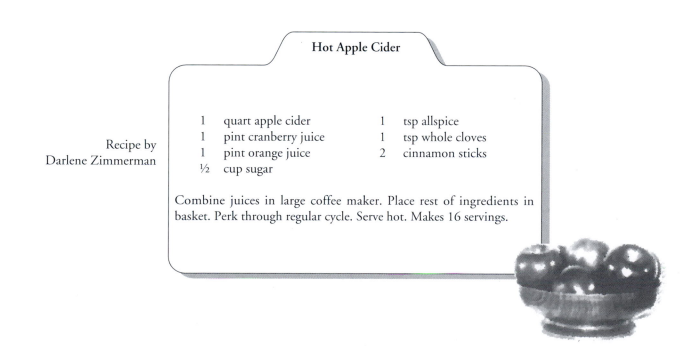

Hot Apple Cider

Recipe by
Darlene Zimmerman

1	quart apple cider	1	tsp allspice
1	pint cranberry juice	1	tsp whole cloves
1	pint orange juice	2	cinnamon sticks
½	cup sugar		

Combine juices in large coffee maker. Place rest of ingredients in basket. Perk through regular cycle. Serve hot. Makes 16 servings.

Beverages

Hot Buttered Rum

½	cup margarine	¾	cup brown sugar
¾	cup powdered sugar	2	cups ice cream

Soften ice cream. Mix ingredients thoroughly and store in freezer. To serve, place 1 heaping tbsp. batter and 1 small jigger white rum in a mug. Fill to top with boiling water.

Just the ticket for those cold winter nights.

Recipe by
Darlene Zimmerman

Recipe by
Darlene Zimmerman

Hot Mulled Cider

2	qts. apple cider	½	cup orange juice
1	tbsp. lemon juice	5	whole cloves
3	tbsp. honey	1	cinnamon stick
½	cup brown sugar		

Combine all ingredients. Simmer for 20 minutes. Serve hot.

Hot Holiday Cranberry Punch

1	32 oz. cranberry juice	3	whole cloves
2	cups orange juice	2	cinnamon sticks
½	cup lemon juice	1	32 oz. ginger ale
¼	cup lime juice		

Mix juices, cloves, and cinnamon sticks. Add ginger ale. Heat.

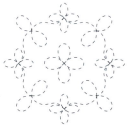

Recipe by
Darlene Zimmerman

Recipe by
Joy Hoffman

Imitation Orange Julius™

6	oz. can frozen orange juice concentrate	¼	cup sugar
		1	tsp. vanilla
1	cup milk	10	ice cubes
1	cup water		

Combine all ingredients in a blender. Blend until smooth (about 30 seconds). Serve immediately. Makes 5-6 cups.

Mexican Hot Chocolate

¼	cup unsweetened cocoa	3	cups milk
2	tbsp. brown sugar	1	tsp. vanilla
1	cup boiling water		whipped cream
¼	tsp. cloves		whole cinnamon sticks
¼	tsp. cinnamon		

Combine cocoa and sugar in a small saucepan. Stir in water. Bring to a boil, reduce heat and cook while stirring for 2 minutes. Add spices and milk. Simmer for 5 minutes. Do not boil. Add vanilla. Serve in mugs, with whipped cream and cinnamon sticks. Makes 4 servings.

Recipe by
Joy Hoffman

Golden Wassail

4	cups unsweetened pineapple juice	1	cup orange juice
1	12 oz. can apricot nectar	1	6" cinnamon stick
4	cups apple cider	1	tsp. whole cloves

Combine all ingredients in a large pan. Heat to boiling and simmer for 15 minutes. Strain into mugs and garnish with thin slices of orange studded with cloves.

Recipe by
Joy Hoffman

Sangria

8	oz. tomato juice	½	tsp. Tabasco Sauce™
4	oz. orange juice	½	tsp. finely chopped onion
1½	tbsp. fresh lime juice		
1½	tbsp. Worcestershire sauce	½	tsp. salt
6	oz. tequila		Cracked ice

Combine juices, Worcestershire sauce, Tabasco Sauce™, onion, and salt with the cracked ice in a blender. Blend and shake. Strain into a small pitcher. Serve tequila in 1 oz. jiggers. Serve Sangria as a chaser.

Recipe by
Maureen Ohland

Russian Tea

½	cup instant tea	½	tsp. cinnamon
1	cup instant orange juice mix	¼	tsp. cloves
		1	pkg. lemonade mix

Mix ingredients together and store in a tightly covered jar. To serve, mix 1-2 tsp. in 1 cup boiling water.

Recipe by
Joy Hoffman

Jello Salad 🍓🍓

17" square

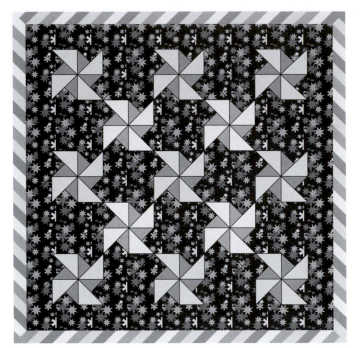

See photograph on page 38.

Versatile, colorful, cool and shimmering. Jello can be any flavor or color of the rainbow. This salad uses clear jewel tones but shouldn't be limited to only these colors. Add a little cream cheese, whipped cream, or even ice cream to this creation and change the colors from deep and rich to smooth and delicate.

Ingredients [1]		
Fabric #1		½ yard large print
Fabric #2		⅛ yard teal
Fabric #3		⅛ yard dark teal
Fabric #4		⅛ yard pink
Fabric #5		⅛ yard dark pink

[1] Optional Candy Cane Binding: Buy ¼ yard of the solids instead of ⅛ yard.

Cutting Directions		
From	Cut	To Get
Fabric #1	1 3½" strip	4 Easy Angle™ triangles
		8 Companion Angle™ triangles
	2 2½" strips	52 - 1½" x 2½" rectangles
	2 1½" strips	52 Easy Angle™ triangles
Fabric #2	2 1½" strips	36 Companion Angle™ triangles
Fabric #3	1 1½" strip	36 Easy Angle™ triangles
Fabric #4	1 1½" strip	16 Companion Angle™ triangles
Fabric #5	1 1½" strip	16 Easy Angle™ triangles

Quilt Assembly

The pinwheels consist of 4 flying geese units and 4 rectangles. Refer to *Basic Ingredients*, page 15, for directions on constructing a flying goose unit. (*Notice the Easy Angle™ triangles are of two different fabrics to achieve the two-dimensional look.*)

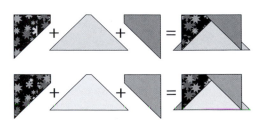

Stitch the rectangles to the top of the flying goose units. Press towards the rectangle.

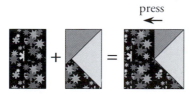

Form the blocks. Pin and match at seam intersections. You will need to make 9 teal blocks and 4 pink blocks.

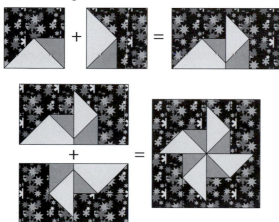

Assemble blocks into diagonal rows, according to diagram. Add the Companion Angle™ and the Easy Angle™ triangles at the beginning and ends of each row. Press the seams in each row all the same direction. The rows can be simply flipped to alternate the seams.

Press, then trim square carefully, allowing a ¼" seam allowance all the way around the quilt as indicated.

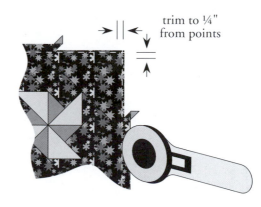

Allow your Jello to set. Hand-quilting was done in the ditch around each of the "marshmallows", and machine meandered in the background area of the quilt for added dimension. Bind with fabric #1 single straight-of-grain binding or the optional candy cane binding.

Optional Candy Cane Binding

Cut a 1½" straight-of-grain strip from each of your 4 solid colored fabrics. Divide each of these strips into 3 equal units (approximately 14"). Join each of these strips in sequence, repeating the sequence until you've used all the strips. As you add on each strip, offset it by 1".

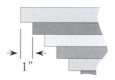

Press the seams all one direction. With your long ruler (e.g., Nancy Crow's Quickline® Ruler), cut 1½" strips at a 45° angle to make bias strips. You should be able to cut 5 of these 1½" bias strips. Join each of these strips to form one long strip for your binding. Add the candy cane binding to your quilt.

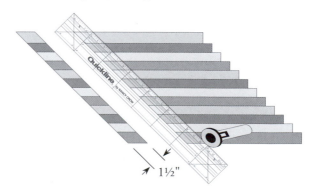

Garden Salad 🌷

54" x 66"

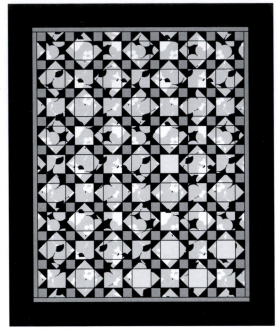

See photograph on page 39.

This Garden Salad has roses in it as well as cool greens – fresh from the garden. You've been admiring those gorgeous English florals, but weren't sure how to use them in a quilt? This is the pattern for you! Notice how the stars that make up the design all flow together? This quilt is put together in rows, rather than blocks, making this pattern very easy to do.

Ingredients		
Fabric #1		1¾ yards large floral
Fabric #2		¾ yards light green
Fabric #3		2½ yards dark green [1]

[1] Includes double straight-of-grain binding

Cutting Directions (7 x 9 setting - 54" x 66")		
From	Cut	To Get
Fabric #1	7 4½" strips 11 2½" strips	63 - 4½" squares 142 Companion Angle™ triangles
Fabric #2	5 2½" strips 5 1½" strips	80 - 2½" squares Inside border
Fabric #3	11 2½" strips 6 5½" strips	284 Easy Angle™ triangles Outside border

Quilt Assembly

Begin by assembling all your flying geese units. You will need to make 142 of them, consisting of fabric #1 for the "goose" and fabric #2 for the background. Refer to *Basic Ingredients*, page 15, for instruction on making the flying goose unit.

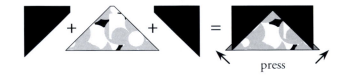

press

Now make 10 of Row A. Notice every other row in the quilt is Row A, and every other Row A is turned upside down as the quilt is constructed. Press as directed.

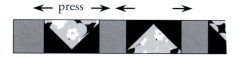

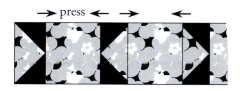

Make 5 of Row B. Follow pressing directions.

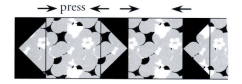

Make 4 of Row C. Follow pressing directions.

Join all the rows, following the sequence shown, ending in an inverted row A. Press all your seams towards Row A.

A
+
B
+
A ↕
+
C
+
A
B
A ↕
C

Add inside and outside borders of fabrics #2 and #3.

We machine quilted this design with EZ International Stitch-Thru™ pattern #6106 in each 4" square, and used #6102 in the border. We quilted horizontal and vertical lines in the ditch.

Bind in double straight-of-grain binding in fabric #3.

Seconds on Garden Salad?

Ingredients	Twin (9 x 13 Setting) 66" x 78"	Full/Queen (15 x 18) 90" x 108"
Fabric #1	3¼ yards large floral	7 yards large floral
Fabric #2	1 yard light green	2 yards light green
Fabric #3	3½ yards dark green [1]	5¾ yards dark green [1]

[1] Includes bias binding

Cutting Directions		
From	Cut	To Get
Twin Size (66" x 78") 9 x 13 Setting		
Fabric #1	13 4½" strips	117 - 4½" squares
	20 2½" strips	256 Companion Angle™ triangles
Fabric #2	9 2½" strips	140 - 2½" squares
	8 1½" strips	Inside border
Fabric #3	20 2½" strips	512 Easy Angle™ triangles
	8 5½" strips	Outside borders
Full/Queen Size (90" x 108") 15 x 18 Setting		
Fabric #1	30 4½" strips	270 - 4½" squares
	45 2½" strips	573 Companion Angle™ triangles
Fabric #2	19 2½" strips	304 - 2½" squares
	10 1½" strips	Inside border
Fabric #3	45 2½" strips	1146 Easy Angle™ triangles
	10 5½" strips	Outside borders

Three Bean & Button Salad 🍅

50" x 62"

See photograph on page 39.

Three Bean Salad was never a favorite salad? Quilters don't do buttons, you say? The Three Bean and Button Salad quilt may change all that for you. Choose a green for the green beans, a gold for the wax beans, and a red for the kidney beans. Add an interesting print or a paisley for a dash of flavor, and you're ready to cut and sew! Mix the ingredients well, sew the blocks together, add borders, then comes the fun part! Raid the ol' button box (or granny's) to discover the treasures hidden there. Your family will have hours of fun choosing favorite buttons to add! Machine-quilt a border design as we did, bind, and your quilt is ready to enjoy for years to come.

Ingredients		
Fabric #1		1½ yards paisley
Fabric #2		1½ yards green [1]
Fabric #3		⅔ yard red
Fabric #4		⅔ yard gold

[1] Includes double straight-of-grain binding

Cutting Directions (4 x 5 setting - 50" x 62")		
From	Cut	To Get
Fabric #1	7 3" strips 5 5½" strips	80 Companion Angle™ triangles [1] Outside borders
Fabric #2	7 3" strips 5 1½" strips	80 Companion Angle™ triangles [1] Inside borders
Fabric #3	7 3" strips	80 Companion Angle™ triangles [1]
Fabric #4	7 3" strips	80 Companion Angle™ triangles [1]

[1] Layer fabric #1 and #2 strips right sides together to cut Companion Angle™ triangles. They will then be ready to chain-sew. Do the same for fabrics #3 and #4.

Quilt Assembly

Chain-sew 80 Half and Half units using the Companion Angle™ triangles from fabrics #1 and #2, with fabric #2 on top. (See *Basic Ingredients*, page 15, for instruction.)

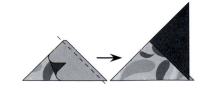

Make 80 more Half and Half units with fabrics #3 and #4, having fabric #3 on top. Press the seams towards the fabric you had on top when sewing.

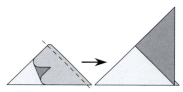

Sew these two different Half and Half units together, making 80 Broken Dishes blocks. (See *Basic Ingredients*, page 15, for instruction.) Press all the seams in the same direction.

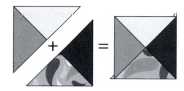

Using 4 units each, assemble 20 blocks with color placement as indicated. Match and pin at each seam intersection. Press as directed.

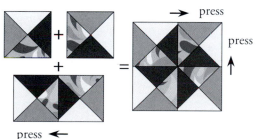

Seconds on Three Bean & Button Salad?

Ingredients	Twin (6 x 9 Setting) 70" x 100"	Queen (8 x 10) 90" x 110"
Fabric #1	3 yards paisley	4 yards paisley
Fabric #2	3 yards green [1]	3⅔ yards green [1]
Fabric #3	1⅔ yards red	2⅓ yards red
Fabric #4	1⅔ yards gold	2⅓ yards gold

[1] Includes double bias binding

Assemble your blocks in five rows of four blocks per row. By rotating the blocks you will be able to alternate seams. Press the seams in each row the same direction, then reverse every other row to make the seams alternate.

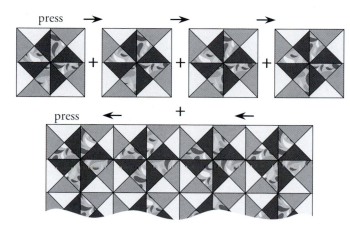

Add simple borders to the quilt.

When your quilt is basted together, you may wish to put in a few lines of machine quilting to hold the layers together. You can then sew buttons at each seam intersection, or at only a few of the seam intersections, through all the layers. It is interesting to have a variety of colors, shapes and sizes of buttons.

Quilt a design in the border. We used EZ International Stitch-Thru™ border design #6104.

Cutting Directions		
From	Cut	To Get
Twin Size (70" x 100") 6 x 9 Setting		
Fabric #1	18 3" strips	216 Companion Angle™ triangles [1]
	9 5½" strips	Outside border
Fabric #2	18 3" strips	216 Companion Angle™ triangles [1]
	8 1½" strips	Inside border
Fabric #3	18 3" strips	216 Companion Angle™ triangles [1]
Fabric #4	18 3" strips	216 Companion Angle™ triangles [1]
Queen Size (90" x 110") 8 x 10 Setting		
Fabric #1	27 3" strips	320 Companion Angle™ triangles [1]
	10 5½" strips	Outside border
Fabric #2	27 3" strips	320 Companion Angle™ triangles [1]
	9 1½" strips	Inside border
Fabric #3	27 3" strips	320 Companion Angle™ triangles [1]
Fabric #4	27 3" strips	320 Companion Angle™ triangles [1]

[1] Layer fabric #1 and #2 strips right sides together to cut Companion Angle™ triangles. They will then be ready to chain-sew. Do the same for fabrics #3 and #4.

Salads

Broccoli Raisin Salad

1	bunch broccoli	1	lb. bacon
½	cup white raisins	1	cup mayonnaise
1	cup sunflower seeds	2	tsp. vinegar
½	cup chopped onion	¼	cup sugar

Break broccoli into small pieces. Cook bacon, drain and crumble. Mix all ingredients together and chill.

Recipe by
Joy Hoffman

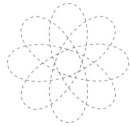

Recipe by
Joy Hoffman

Summer Sauerkraut Salad

1	16 oz. can sauerkraut	½	cup sugar
½	cup each of red and green pepper	¼	tsp. salt
		⅛	tsp. pepper
1	small onion	2	cups chopped celery

Drain and rinse sauerkraut. Combine all ingredients and chill.

Cauliflower Salad

2	cups salad dressing	1	head cauliflower
⅓	cup Parmesan cheese	1	head cabbage, shredded
⅓	cup sugar	1	small onion
¼	tsp. salt	1	lb. bacon
½	tsp. pepper		

Shred cabbage. Chop onion finely. Cook, drain, and crumble bacon. Combine cauliflower, cabbage, and onion. Combine remaining ingredients to make the dressing. Add the bacon. Serve well chilled.

Recipe by
Joy Hoffman

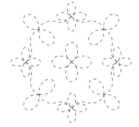

Recipe by
Elda Schefus

German Potato Salad

4	slices bacon	⅓	cup vinegar
1	small onion	⅔	cup water
2	tbsp. flour	½	tsp. salt
⅓	cup sugar		Potatoes

Dice onion and bacon. Fry bacon, adding onion when half done. When bacon is completely done, add remaining ingredients and bring to a boil. Pour over hot, cooked, sliced potatoes.

Frog-eye Salad

1	cup sugar	2	20 oz. cans chunk pineapple
2	tbsp. flour	1	20 oz. can crushed pineapple
½	tsp. salt	1	9 oz. container whipped topping
1¾	cups pineapple juice		
2	eggs	1	cup miniature marshmallows
1	tbsp. lemon juice		
1	box Acini de Pepe pasta	1	cup coconut (optional)
3	11 oz. cans mandarin oranges		

Continued on next card.

Recipe by
Darlene Zimmerman

Continued.

Beat eggs. Combine sugar, flour, and salt. Add pineapple juice and beaten eggs. Cook until thickened. Add lemon juice. Cool. Cook pasta until done. Drain and rinse. Add cooled, cooked mixture. *Refrigerate overnight.* Drain fruit and add fruit, whipped topping, marshmallows, and (if you like) coconut.

This is a great salad to feed a crowd. It can be kept in the refrigerator as long as a week, or it can be frozen.

Recipe by
Darlene Zimmerman

Apple Salad

4	green apples	Salad dressing
4	red apples	Bananas
1	can chunk pineapple	Marshmallows

Core the apples, but do not peel. Cut into chunks. Drain pineapple and add. Mix apples and pineapple with enough salad dressing to coat. *Refrigerate overnight.* Add sliced bananas and/or marshmallows before serving.

Frozen Delight Salad

1	cup sugar	1	can crushed pineapple
2	cups water	1	container frozen strawberries in syrup
3	bananas		
1	can apricots		

Thaw strawberries. Warm water. Dissolve sugar in water. Mix fruits and pour sugar water over fruits. Pour into a cake pan and freeze. Cut into squares to serve. You may also freeze in individual portions in paper-lined muffin tins. When frozen, pop out and serve.

Recipe by
Sharon Hultgren

Porcupines ❀❀❀

63½" x 88"

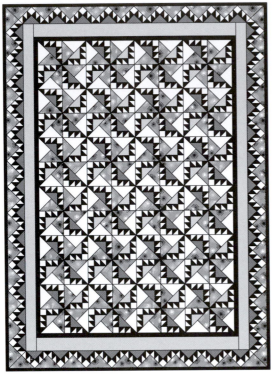

This striking quilt, accented in black, reminds us of those tasty little meatballs studded with rice. The quilt is perfect for anyone looking for a masculine design.

We've done this quilt in a feminine version also, with white, pink and lavender fabrics and plain borders.

Ingredients		
Fabric #1		1¾ yards print
Fabric #2		1⅛ yards blue
Fabric #3		¾ yard rust
Fabric #4		2½ yards background
Fabric #5		2¾ yards black [1]

[1] Includes 1 yard for double bias binding.

See photograph on page 40.

Cutting Directions [1]		
From	Cut	To Get
Fabric #1	11 3½" strips	96 Companion Angle™ triangles [2]
Fabric #2	4 2⅝" strips	48 Companion Angle™ triangles
	4 3¼" strips	Second border [3]
	3 3½" strips	Second border [3]
Fabric #3	4 2⅝" strips	48 Companion Angle™ triangles
Fabric #4	18 2" strips	96 squares
		384 Easy Angle™ triangles [4]
	11 3½" strips	96 Companion Angle™ triangles [2]
Fabric #5	13 2" strips	384 Easy Angle™ triangles [4]
	9 1⅝" strips	192 Companion Angle™ triangles
	6 1½" strips	First border

[1] Use leftovers from this table when cutting pieced border (table on page 66).

[2] Layer fabrics right sides together and cut Companion Angle™ triangles. They will then be ready to chain-sew.

[3] Cut in two sizes with the short sides being slightly wider to allow the pieced border to fit. Adjust this border to make the outside border fit. *Do not cut these strips until you have pieced the body of the quilt.*

[4] Layer fabrics right sides together and cut Easy Angle™ triangles. They will then be ready to chain-sew into triangle squares.

Quilt Assembly

Begin by assembling all the Easy Angle™ triangle squares. (See *Basic Ingredients*, page 15, for instruction.) Stack press towards the dark triangles.

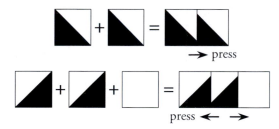

Sew half the triangle squares into these units of two and the other half into units of two facing the opposite direction. Add a plain square to these latter units. Press seams as shown.

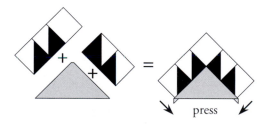

Add these units to the sides of your fabric #2 and #3 triangles. Press towards the large triangle. You will need to make 96 of these units, 48 with fabric #2 and 48 with fabric #3.

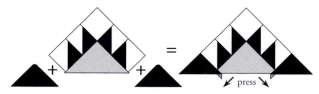

Finish these units by adding fabric #5 triangles at both ends of the triangle.

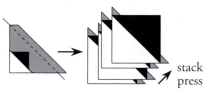

Sew the large fabric #1 and #4 Companion Angle™ triangles together to form a Half and Half unit (see *Basic Ingredients*, page 15, for instructions), having fabric #1 on top. Press seam towards the darkest triangle.

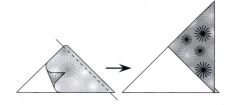

Add these to your previous units to make 96 blocks. Press towards the larger triangles. *You may need to sew a slightly larger seam allowance to make your points come out nicely.*

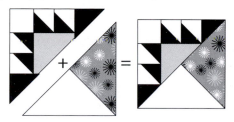

Finish a 12" block by stitching 4 of these pieced squares together. Alternate seams. You need to make 24 of these blocks.

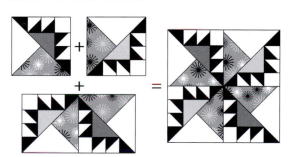

Join these blocks in a 4 block by 6 block setting for the body of the quilt.

Borders

Add the simple border of fabric #5 to the quilt body. At this point measure your quilt, raw edge to raw edge, and adjust your fabric #2 borders to yield a quilt that measures 56" x 68½", raw edges to raw edges.

The pieced border requires 44 of these units, pieced in the same manner as for your blocks. The larger triangles are from fabric #3.

Main Dishes

Add a fabric #5 Companion Angle™ triangle to the right side of 40 units. Add a fabric #1 Companion Angle™ triangle to the left side of the unit. Construct 40 of these units.

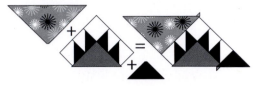

Add fabric #1 Companion Angles™ to both sides of the remaining 4 units. These are used in the corners.

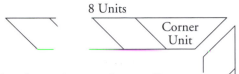

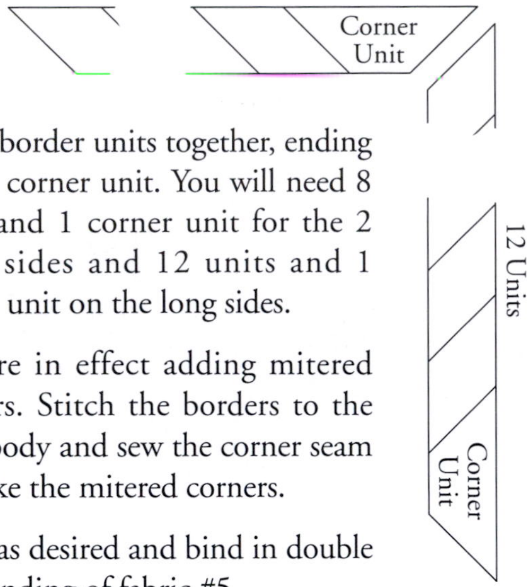

Stitch border units together, ending with a corner unit. You will need 8 units and 1 corner unit for the 2 short sides and 12 units and 1 corner unit on the long sides.

You are in effect adding mitered borders. Stitch the borders to the quilt body and sew the corner seam to make the mitered corners.

Quilt as desired and bind in double bias binding of fabric #5.

The table below shows cutting requirements for the pieced border.

Cutting Directions - Pieced Border [1]		
From	Cut	To Get
Fabric #1	6 3⅝" strips	48 Companion Angle™ triangles
Fabric #3	4 2⅝" strips	44 Companion Angle™ triangles
Fabric #4	5 2" strips	44 squares 88 Easy Angle™ triangles [2]
Fabric #5	3 2" strips 2 1⅝" strips	88 Easy Angle™ triangles [2] 40 Companion Angle™ triangles

[1] Fabric requirements are included in the Ingredients table on page 64.
[2] Layer fabrics right sides together and cut Easy Angle™ triangles. They will then be ready to chain-sew.

Pink Porcupines
71½" x 95½"

See photograph on page 41.

Ingredients	
Fabric #1	2¾ yards print
Fabric #2	2 yards lavender [1]
Fabric #3	½ yard pink
Fabric #4	3⅛ yards background
Fabric #5	2 yards dark purple

[1] Includes 1 yard for double bias binding.

Cutting Directions		
From	Cut	To Get
Fabric #1	16 3½" strips 8 4½" strips	140 Companion Angle™ triangles [1] Outside border
Fabric #2	6 2⅝" strips 8 2" strips	70 Companion Angle™ triangles Inside border
Fabric #3	6 2⅝" strips	70 Companion Angle™ triangles
Fabric #4	16 3½" strips 26 2" strips	140 Companion Angle™ triangles [1] 560 Easy Angle™ triangles [2] 140 squares
Fabric #5	19 2" strips 14 1⅝" strips	560 Easy Angle™ triangles [2] 280 Companion Angle™ triangles

[1] Layer fabrics right sides together and cut Companion Angle™ triangles. They will then be ready to chain-sew.
[2] Layer fabrics right sides together and cut Easy Angle™ triangles. They will then be ready to chain-sew into triangle squares.

Christmas Goose ✸

30" Square

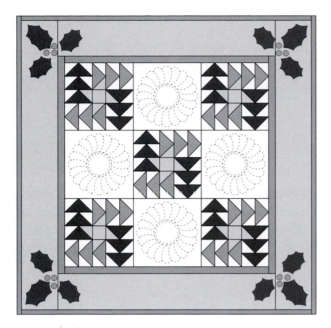

See photograph on page 42.

"Christmas Goose" was at one time a family tradition (and still is for some). Now most no longer follow that tradition, preferring to eat turkey instead. We wanted to make a special Christmas wall hanging with the "flavor" of those bygone Christmas feasts, and this "Christmas Goose" quilt is the result. The pattern is given in three sizes: miniature (10" square), 30" square, or 42" square, depending on the size of your appetite!

Ingredients		
Fabric #1		½ yard red [1]
Fabric #2		¼ yard green
Fabric #3		½ yard background
Fabric #4		⅔ yard brown

[1] Includes straight-of-grain binding

Cutting Directions		
From	Cut	To Get
Fabric #1	2 2" strips	30 Companion Angle™ triangles
	4 1¼" strips	Inside border
	1 1½" strip	12 circles for berries [1]
Fabric #2	2 2" strips	30 Companion Angle™ triangles
	1 3" strip	4 large and 8 small leaves with templates
Fabric #3	4 2" strips	100 Easy Angle™ triangles
	1 8" strip	4 - 8" squares
Fabric #4	1 2" strip	20 Easy Angle™ triangles
		5 - 2" squares
	4 4½" strips	Outside border

[1] Circles are cut with a quarter for a template, marked directly on the wrong side of fabric #1. Use this size for *stuffed* berries; use a smaller coin for flat berries.

Quilt Assembly

Begin by assembling 40 flying geese units, 20 each using fabric #1 and #2 Companion Angle™ triangles with fabric #3 Easy Angle™ triangles. Then make 10 each using fabric #1 and #2

Companion Angle™ triangles with fabric #3 Easy Angle™ triangles on the left and fabric #4 Easy Angle™ triangles on the right. See *Basic Ingredients*, page 15, for piecing the Flying Geese units.

Make 20   Make 20   Make 10   Make 10

Assemble 10 top and bottom sections for the 5 blocks. Then assemble the 5 center sections.

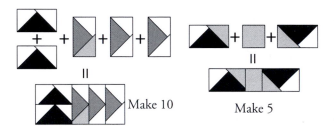

Make 10   Make 5

Combine these units to make the 5 blocks.

Add fabric #3 setting squares between blocks as shown in the graphic. Press towards the plain blocks. (Note: If your pieced blocks aren't exactly 8",

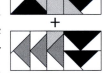

cut your plain blocks the same measurement as your pieced blocks.)

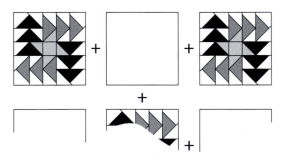

Sew inside border of fabric #1 to outside border of fabric #4. Press towards the outside border. Add borders to the four sides of the quilt, mitering corners. (See page 21.)

Appliquéd Corners

You may use any method of appliqué you choose. The freezer paper method is what I feel most comfortable using. For this method you need *white* freezer paper, available in most grocery stores. The wax will adhere the paper to your fabric with the heat of your iron. Trace the leaf template onto your freezer paper (the paper side) as many times as needed. Notice that no seam allowances are added. Cut out the paper templates on the pencil line. Then iron the waxy side of each template onto your fabric, allowing enough space for seam allowances. By eye, cut your leaves out of the fabric, adding ⅛" + turn-under allowance as you are cutting. Baste each leaf in place. When the leaves are sewn down, slit the back of the quilt top behind each leaf and pull out the paper.

To make the berries, baste ⅛" inside of each circle with single matching thread. Pull basting thread to form an open pouch. Stuff tightly with batting. (*Tip: Cotton batting works best.*) Pull basting thread tighter, then run another line of basting, and pull tighter again. Secure by stitching across the opening from several directions. Finally, appliqué the little ball in place. As an option for the berries you might cover buttons with fabric #3, or simply use red buttons, or even appliqué a smaller flat circle.

Berries could be appliquéd in place first, or you may add them *after* the quilting is done. Appliqué the large central leaf over the mitered seam. Add a smaller leaf on each side of it. The berries and leaves don't need to be perfectly identical or perfectly placed on each corner. They aren't identical in nature, and remember, you are creating a piece of "folk-art".

Because the quilt is so traditional in form, you may choose to quilt it heavily by hand. The quilt shown is quilted in each "goose" and ¼" inside the center star. A very traditional feather wreath is quilted in each of the plain blocks. The border was cross-hatched in 1" squares on the diagonal. Quilting was done around each leaf, and the veins of the leaves were quilted.

Bind in single straight-of grain binding of fabric #1.

Don't forget to sign and date your quilt – it will be a family heirloom!

Christmas Gosling

Construct this miniature quilt using the same approach as for the larger quilt, but substituting the Christmas fabric for the brown in the border, and the gold fabric for the brown in the goose blocks.

Christmas Gosling Ingredients - 10" Square
Fabric #1 - ¼ yard red [1]
Fabric #2 - ¼ yard green [1]
Fabric #3 - ¼ yard background [1]
Fabric #4 - ¼ yard Christmas print [1]
Fabric #5 - Gold scraps

[1] Yardage or scraps.

See photograph on page 42.

Christmas Gosling Cutting Directions - 10" Square		
From	Cut	To Get
Fabric #1	2 1" strips	30 Companion Angle™ triangles Inside border
Fabric #2	1 1" strip	30 Companion Angle™ triangles
Fabric #3	2 1" strips 1 3" strip	100 Easy Angle™ triangles 4 - 3" squares
Fabric #4	1 2" strip	Outside border
Fabric #5	1 1" strip	20 Easy Angle™ triangles 5 - 1" square

Seconds on Christmas Goose?

Ingredients - 42" Square		
Fabric #1		⅔ yard red [1]
Fabric #2		⅜ yard green
Fabric #3		⅔ yard background
Fabric #4		⅞ yard brown

[1] Includes single binding, or buy 1 yard for double binding.

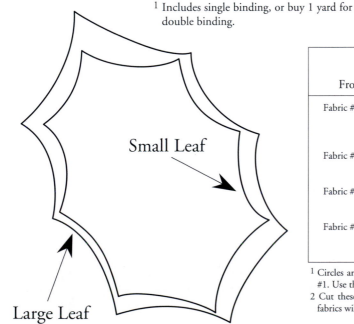

Small Leaf

Large Leaf

Cutting Directions - 42" Square		
From	Cut	To Get
Fabric #1	3 2½" strips 4 1½" strips 1 1½" strip	30 Companion Angle™ triangles Inside border 12 circles for berries [1]
Fabric #2	3 2½" strips 1 3½" strip	30 Companion Angle™ triangles 12 large leaves cut with templates
Fabric #3	4 2½" strips 1 10½" strip	100 Easy Angle™ triangles 4 - 10½" squares
Fabric #4	2 2½" strips 4 5½" strips	20 Easy Angle™ triangles 5 - 2½" squares Outside borders [2]

[1] Circles are cut with a quarter for a template, marked directly on the wrong side of fabric #1. Use this size for *stuffed* berries; use a smaller coin for flat berries.

[2] Cut these borders a little narrower if needed to allow you to use one strip per border; fabrics will vary in width.

California Hotdish 🍎

47½" x 60" (4" Block)

See photograph on page 42.

Joy's sister-in-law, another native Californian, truly appreciates all the natural beauty as well as the delightful personalities the state of Minnesota offers. The one thing, however, that provides her with infinite merriment is the term "hotdish" which has been defined as "any number of bland ingredients held together with cream-of-something soup and baked entirely too long".

The California Hotdish quilt began as an all-out effort to dispel the myth that food in Minnesota is

Ingredients		
Fabric #1		1⅓ yards party print
Fabric #2		1 yard (total) various solid prints
Fabric #3		¼ yard accent (any one of the prints)
Fabric #4		1¼ yards solid [1]
Fabric #5		¾ yard (can be any of the above) [2]

[1] For setting squares and half-squares
[2] For double bias binding (½ yard for straight-of-grain)

dull. This "hotdish" uses crisp, snappy colors and a simple block tossed together lightly for a quilt that is anything but bland. Vary the "ingredients" as much or as little as you like. Remember, "California Hotdish" can be any combination from wild to tame – choose as few as three colors or use up "leftovers" to create a design as unique or as traditional as you please. You may chose to halve, double, or triple the recipe to change the size.

Cutting Directions		
From	Cut	To Get
Fabric #1	10 2½" strips 6 3½" strips	126 Companion Angle™ triangles Outside border
Fabric #2	10 2½" strips	126 Companion Angle™ triangles
Fabric #3	5 1½" strips	Inside border
Fabric #4	6 4½" strips 4 3½" strips	48 setting squares 28 Companion Angle™ triangles 4 Easy Angle™ triangles

Quilt Assembly

Refer to *Basic Ingredients*, page 15, for instructions on making the Broken Dishes block from fabric #1 and coordinating fabric #2 triangles. You need 63 Broken Dishes blocks.

Assemble in diagonal rows. Mix the Broken Dishes blocks well, randomly turning blocks for

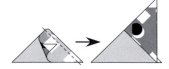

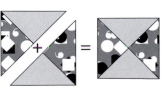

a casual look. Refer to the graphic, or the photograph on page 42 for placement.

Add simple borders of fabrics #3 and #1.

Top with a quilted motif in the plain blocks; we used Stitch-Thru™ Tear-Away Stencil pattern #6106, "Pumpkin Seed". Quilt the diagonal lines in the Broken Dishes blocks. We finished with Stitch-Thru™ Tear-Away Stencil border design #6102 for the border.

Seconds on California Hotdish?

Ingredients	Twin (10 x 15 Setting) 63" x 87"	Full/Queen (13 x 16) 86" x 103"
Fabric #1	3¼ yards party print	4¼ yards
Fabric #2	2 yards (total) various solid prints	2½ yards (total)
Fabric #3	⅜ yard accent (any one of the prints)	½ yard
Fabric #4	2½ yards solid [1]	3½ yards [1]
Fabric #5	¾ yard (can be any of the above) [2]	1 yard [2]

[1] For setting squares and half-squares
[2] For double bias binding

Cutting Directions		
From	**Cut**	**To Get**
Twin Size (63" x 87") 10 x 15 Setting		
Fabric #1	24 2½" strips	300 Companion Angle™ triangles
	8 6½" strips	Outside border
Fabric #2	24 2½" strips	300 Companion Angle™ triangles
Fabric #3	8 1½" strips	Inside border
Fabric #4	14 4½" strips	126 setting squares
	6 3½" strips	46 Companion Angle™ triangles
		4 Easy Angle™ triangles
Full/Queen Size (86" x 103") 13 x 16 Setting		
Fabric #1	32 2½" strips	416 Companion Angle™ triangles
	10 6½" strips	Outside border
Fabric #2	32 2½" strips	416 Companion Angle™ triangles
Fabric #3	10 1½" strips	Inside border
Fabric #4	20 4½" strips	180 setting squares
	7 3½" strips	54 Companion Angle™ triangles
		4 Easy Angle™ triangles

Beef Burgundy

60" x 80" (18 Pieced Blocks)

See photograph on page 43.

Beef Burgundy is simply the Mint Julep block (page 50) made larger and set on point with sashing. With the rich colors we've chosen, it makes a very dramatic statement. Most of this quilt was machine quilted, but hand quilting was added in the plain half-blocks for a special touch. This is a nice way to combine the speed of machine quilting and showcase the beauty of hand quilting in the plain half blocks.

Ingredients		
Fabric #1		2 yards cream
Fabric #2		2 yards navy [1]
Fabric #3		1¼ yards print
Fabric #4		1⅓ yards burgundy

[1] Includes ¾ yards for double bias binding

Cutting Directions		
From	**Cut**	**To Get**
Fabric #1	10 3" strips	72 Companion Angle™ triangles [1]
		72 Easy Angle™ triangles
	2 18½" strips	3 - 18½" squares for 10 half-block triangles [2]
		2 - 10½" squares for 4 corner triangles [3]
Fabric #2	9 4" strips	72 Companion Angle™ triangles
	2 2" strips	31 squares
Fabric #3	6 3" strips	72 Companion Angle™ triangles [1]
	7 3½" strips	Outside border
Fabric #4	12 2" strips	48 - 2" x 10½" sashing strips
	7 2" strips	Inside border

[1] Layer strips right sides together and cut. They will then be ready to chain sew.
[2] Cut squares across both diagonals (see page 14).
[3] Cut squares across one diagonal (see page 14).

Quilt Assembly

Assemble the blocks in the same fashion as for the Mint Julep block (page 51). First, chain-sew

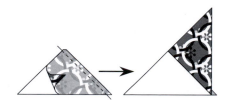

the Companion Angle™ triangles. Then construct the Cream at the Top units. Attach

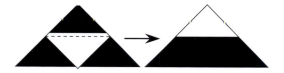

these two sets of units in pairs and combine sets of four to form the blocks.

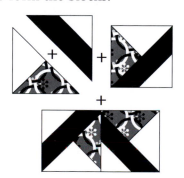

Add sashing between blocks, add the large half block triangles, and set the blocks and rows together on the diagonal, adding the corner triangles last, following the graphic for placement.

Add borders, simple or mitered. The entire center of the quilt was machine stitched in the ditch. We added a hand-quilted motif in each of the half block triangles, and used Stitch-Thru™ Tear-Away Stencil design #6101 in the border.

Bind in double bias binding.

Cutting Directions (82" x 113") 4 x 6 Setting - 39 Pieced Blocks		
From	Cut	To Get
Fabric #1	21 3" strips	156 Companion Angle™ triangles [1]
		156 Easy Angle™ triangles
	2 18½" strips	4 - 18½" squares for 16 half-block triangles [2]
	1 10½" strips	2 - 10½" squares for 4 corner triangles [3]
Fabric #2	20 4" strips	156 Companion Angle™ triangles
	3 2" strips	58 squares
Fabric #3	13 3" strips	156 Companion Angle™ triangles [1]
	17 4½" strips	First and third borders [4]
Fabric #4	24 2" strips	96 - 2" x 10½" sashing strips
	8 2" strips	Second border [4]

Seconds on Beef Burgundy?

Ingredients (82" x 113")		
Fabric #1		3¼ yards cream
Fabric #2		3¾ yards navy [1]
Fabric #3		3¼ yards print
Fabric #4		2 yards burgundy

[1] Includes 1¼ yards for double bias binding

[1] Layer strips right sides together and cut. They will then be ready to chain sew.
[2] Cut squares across both diagonals (see page 14).
[3] Cut squares across one diagonal (see page 14).
[4] Finished borders are (1) 4" print, (2) 1½" burgundy, and (3) 4" print.

Main Dishes

Holiday Porcupines

1½ lbs. ground beef
½ cup uncooked rice
¼ cup half and half or evaporated milk
½ cup chopped onion
1 egg
Salt and pepper

1 10½ oz. can tomato soup
½ soup can water
¼ cup chopped onion
1 tsp. Worcestershire sauce
½ tsp. garlic salt

Continued on next card.

Recipe by Joy Hoffman

See related quilt recipe on page 64.

Continued

Thoroughly mix ground beef, uncooked rice, half and half, onion, egg, and salt and pepper (to taste). Shape the mixture into walnut sized balls. Fry the meatballs in a little oil in a skillet, turning to brown evenly. Or, place on a baking pan and bake at 350° until brown (approximately 15 minutes.) Mix and heat together the remaining ingredients. Add the browned meatballs to the sauce. Cover with a tight fitting lid and simmer over low heat for 45 minutes. Pour into a serving dish, garnish with chopped chives and serve at once. Makes 6-7 portions, or about 2½ dozen porcupines.

California Hotdish

1½ lbs. ground beef
1 clove garlic, minced
1 tsp. salt
1 large onion, finely chopped
1 green pepper, chopped
1 tsp. chili powder
2½ cups tomatoes (#2 can)

1 #303 can red kidney beans
¾ cup uncooked rice
½ cup chopped ripe olives
¾ cup grated aged Cheddar cheese

Continued on next card.

Recipe by Joy Hoffman

See related quilt recipe on page 70.

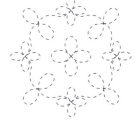

Unlike a Minnesota hotdish, this recipe doesn't have cream-of-anything soup in it!

Continued

Brown meat quickly in a large skillet, reduce heat and add garlic, salt, onion, green pepper, and chili powder. Cover and cook until vegetables are limp, but not brown. Turn off heat. Lightly grease a large casserole dish. Place the meat mixture in the dish, then pour in the tomatoes, kidney beans, uncooked rice, and olives (include juices from cans). Blend with a spatula, being careful not to mash the beans. Bake at 350° for 1 hour. Top with cheese and bake 25 minutes more. If the mixture appears a bit dry, add three tablespoons of tomato juice. Makes 8-10 servings.

Hot Turkey Sandwich Filling

6	cups cooked, cut-up turkey	¾	cup (or less) chopped onion
1	cup mayonnaise		
1½	cups chopped celery	1	can cream of mushroom soup
Seasoning to taste			

Mix ingredients together. Bake 30-45 minutes at 350°. The longer the baking time, the better the taste.

Recipe by
Joy Hoffman

Cashew Chicken

5	oz. chow mein noodles	1	can cream of mushroom soup
2	cups diced, cooked chicken		
¾	cup chopped celery	1	cup cashew nuts
½	cup green onion	¾	cup chicken broth

Combine all ingredients (reserving a few chow mein noodles) and place in a greased 2 quart casserole dish. Sprinkle remaining noodles over top. Bake at 325° for 30 minutes.

Recipe by
Darlene Zimmerman

Beef Bergundy

2-3	lbs. sirloin steak, cubed	Celery salt to taste	
3	cans beef consommé	Cooking oil	
1	tbsp. soy sauce	Burgundy wine to taste	
2	cloves garlic, crushed	2	tbsp. cornstarch
Onion salt to taste		Rice or noodles	

Recipe by
Maureen Ohland

See related quilt
recipe on page 72.

Brown steak slowly in oil. Mix consommé, soy sauce, garlic, onion salt, and celery salt in a bowl and add to browned meat. Simmer at least 1 hour. Add wine in small amounts while simmering. Fifteen minutes before serving, thicken with water thinned cornstarch. Serve over rice or noodles.

Quilter's Oven Beef Stew

1½	lbs. stew meat (unbrowned)	2	cups beef boullion
2	cups diced potatoes	1	cup tomato juice
6	medium carrots, chunked	1	tbsp. sugar
1	cup celery	2	tbsp. cornstarch or tapioca
1	large onion		

Mix all ingredients in a large oven container. Bake at 250° for 5 hours. *Do not peek.*

Recipe by
Darlene Zimmerman

Bread Pudding 🍎

42" x 56" (14" Block)

See photographs on page 43 and cover.

This pattern is based on an old pattern named "Lady of the Lake", and it's much easier than it looks. You could make this lovely quilt with the warm-toned scraps of "old" fabrics you have on hand – simply sort them into lights or darks to make the Bread Pudding version of this pattern. Add a few raisins and a bit of cinnamon for color and interest and enjoy a warm and toasty quilt.

Ingredients – (3 x 4 Block Setting)	
Fabric #1	¼ yard each of at least 12 darks [1]
Fabric #2	¼ yard of at least 12 lights [2]

[1] Use scraps or yardage (a total of approximately 3 yards) of a mixture of prints, checks, plaids; from black, brown, gray, dark blue, and rusty red.

[2] Use scraps or yardage (a total of approximately 3 yards) of a mixture of prints, checks, plaids; from off-white, tan, gold, light browns, and light blues.

Cutting Directions (3 x 4 Block Setting)		
From	Cut	To Get
Fabric #1	1 4¾" strip [1] 2½" strips	2 Companion Angle™ triangles from each dark [2] 32 Easy Angle™ triangles from each dark [2]
Fabric #2	1 4¾" strip [1] 2½" strips	2 Companion Angle™ triangles from each light [2] 32 Easy Angle™ triangles from each light [2]

[1] Use remainder of strip to cut short 2½" strips for Easy Angle™ triangles

[2] Based on 12 fabrics each of lights and darks. More fabrics will require fewer pieces per fabric, as long as the total for each value (light/dark) is the same.

Quilt Assembly

After cutting the Easy Angle™ triangles, set aside 4 lights and 4 darks for each block (48 of each for a 3 x 4 block setting). Then pair each remaining light triangle (randomly selected) with one remaining dark. Then chain sew to

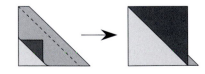

make 28 triangle squares for each block (336 for a 3 x 4 block setting).

Each block will be made from four units. Make predominately dark units from seven randomly selected triangle squares, one randomly selected large dark Companion Angle™ triangle, and two of the dark triangles set aside earlier. Make two units per block (a total of 24 for the 3 x 4 block setting).

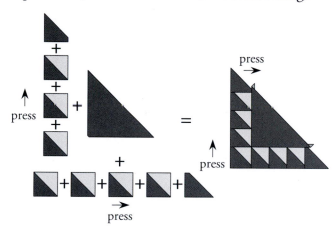

Make a similar set of two predominately light units per block from seven randomly selected triangle squares, a randomly selected large light triangle, and two of the light triangles set aside earlier.

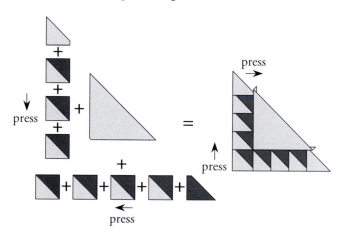

After all of these units are constructed, lay them out in a pleasing manner, with two light and two dark units per block, alternate the units within each block and then alternate the orientation of the blocks as shown. Sew the blocks together in a 3 x 4 setting.

Quilt in the ditch along the diagonal seams and add an interesting motif in the center squares, such as EZ International Stitch-Thru™ designs #6106, # 6107, #6108, or #6109.

Bind in either a bias or straight-of-grain binding. We have used a small plaid in a bias binding to give an interesting effect.

Ingredients – Full/Queen – 84" x 98" (6 x 7 Block Setting)		
Fabric #1	▓	½ yard each of at least 12 darks [1]
Fabric #2	░	½ yard of at least 12 lights [2]

[1] Use yardage or scraps (scraps should total approximately 6 yards) of a mixture of prints, checks, plaids; from black, brown, gray, dark blue, and rusty red.

[2] Use yardage or scraps (scraps should total approximately 6 yards) of a mixture of prints, checks, plaids; from off-white, tan, gold, light browns, and light blues.

Seconds on Bread Pudding?

Cutting Directions – Full/Queen – 84" x 98" (6 x 7 Block Setting)		
From	Cut	To Get
Fabric #1	1 4¾" strip [1] 2½" strips	7 Companion Angle™ triangles from each dark [2] 112 Easy Angle™ triangles from each dark [2]
Fabric #2	1 4¾" strip [1] 2½" strips	7 Companion Angle™ triangles from each light [2] 112 Easy Angle™ triangles from each light [2]

[1] Cut from 1 strip. If necessary, cut an extra 4¾" piece (not a whole strip).

[2] Based on 12 fabrics each of lights and darks.

For Blueberry Freeze, collect as many blues and whites as your imagination allows and create a frozen treat, sure to delight everyone. Again, simply sort the fabrics into lights and darks.

Blueberry Freeze

See photograph on page 44.

Blueberry Freeze Ingredients (4 x 5 Block Setting)		
Fabric #1	▓	⅓ yard each of at least 12 dark blue prints [1]
Fabric #2	░	⅓ yard of at least 12 light blue/white prints [1]

[1] Use yardage or scraps (scraps should total approximately 4 yards of dark blue prints and 4 yards of light blue/white prints).

Blueberry Freeze Cutting Directions (4 x 5 Block Setting)		
From	Cut	To Get
Fabric #1	1 4¾" strip [1] 2½" strips	3 or 4 Companion Angle™ triangles from each dark [2] 53 or 54 Easy Angle™ triangles from each dark [2]
Fabric #2	1 4¾" strip [1] 2½" strips	3 or 4 Companion Angle™ triangles from each light [2] 53 or 54 Easy Angle™ triangles from each light [2]

[1] Use remainder of strip to cut short 2½" strips for Easy Angle™ triangles

[2] Based on 12 fabrics each of lights and darks. Cut 3 large triangles for 8 of each value, and 4 for the other 4 of each value. Cut 53 Easy Angle™ Triangles for 8 of each value and 54 for the other 4 of each value.

Black Forest Torte ❦❦❦

28" x 38"

See photograph on page 45.

Sometimes it's interesting to choose a name for a quilt and then make the quilt to fit the name. It's a new approach to quilt designing, and may open up some of your creativity. For Black Forest Torte you of course need to use the colors of dark chocolate, cherries and cream; but the name also makes you think of the real Black Forest, which means pine trees. Starting with a gorgeous Christmas print, we've designed a quilt with all these ingredients, and a few extra surprises! Look closely at the trees in the photograph (page 45) and you can see a gold star at the top of each tree, and beads sewn on in clusters to decorate the trees. These little touches can make your quilt that extra special dessert!

Ingredients

Fabric #1		⅔ yard background
Fabric #2		¼ yard green
Fabric #3		Gold or brown scraps
Fabric #4		⅝ yard black [1]
Fabric #5		Red scraps
Fabric #6		⅞ yard Christmas print

[1] Includes straight-of-grain binding

Cutting Directions

From	Cut	To Get
Fabric #1	8 1½" strips	64 - 4" trapezoids [1]
		16 - 1½" x 3" rectangles
	2 4" strips	32 Easy Angle™ triangles
Fabric #2	3 1½" strips	8 Companion Angle™ triangles
		8 - 3" trapezoids [2]
		16 - 4" trapezoids [1]
Fabric #3	1 1½" strip	8 - 1½" squares
Fabric #4	5 1" strips	Sashing around tree blocks
	4 1" strips	Second border
Fabric #5	4 1" strips	First border
Fabric #6	2 5½" strips	6 Companion Angle™ triangles (half blocks)
		4 Easy Angle II™ triangles (corner triangles)
	4 4" strips	Outside border

[1] The base of the trapezoid should fall on the solid line below the 4" dashed line of Companion Angle™, as if you were cutting a 4" finished size triangle (See page 10).

[2] The base of the trapezoid should fall on the solid line below the 3" dashed line of Companion Angle™, as if you were cutting a 3" finished size triangle (See page 10).

Quilt Assembly

With your Easy Angle™ trim off the "dog-ears" on both sides of the tree triangles and trapezoids. This will make it much easier to

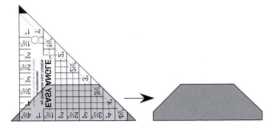

position the background trapezoids. Add background trapezoids to tree triangles and trapezoids. Press seams towards the tree.

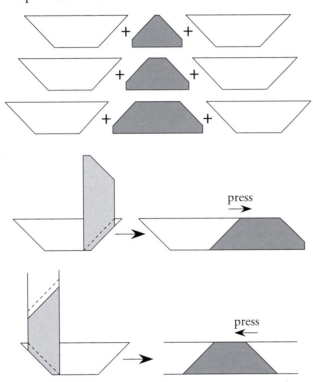

Add background rectangles to the tree trunks. Press towards the trunks.

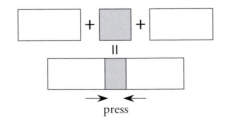

Crease each tree triangle or trapezoid in the center. Use this crease to center each strip of the

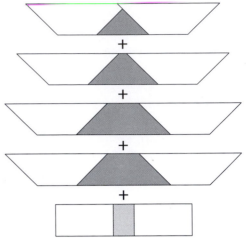

tree as you assemble the tree, starting from the top down. When all your tree blocks are complete, press the seams going down the tree. Now trim each tree block to 5". If the block is too long, trim off the bottom of the block.

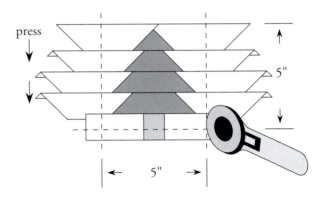

Add the background Easy Angle™ triangles to the top and bottom of your tree blocks. Press towards the block, then add Easy Angle™ triangles to both sides. Press again and trim each block to 6¾" square.

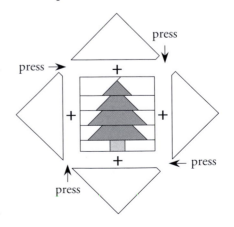

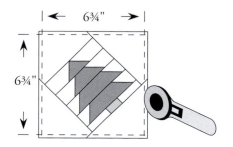

6¾"

6¾"

Set tree blocks together with sashing strips and the large Christmas print triangles. Follow piecing sequence. Press all seams towards sashing strips.

Sew together all three of your borders, fabrics #5, #4 , and #6, in that order. Press towards the fabric #6 border.

Add mitered borders to your quilt. (See *Finishing Your Quilt*, page 21.)

The quilt shown was quilted entirely by machine. Each of the trees was stitched in the ditch as well as on both sides of the sashing and borders. A small meander was done in the background behind the trees, and a larger meander was done in the Christmas print triangles and in the outside border. Gold metallic stars were pressed on to the top of each tree. EZ International Cross-Locked beads were pulled off the string and sewn on, one at a time by hand, in a cluster of three, at random intervals.

Bind in fabric #4 in double or single straight-of-grain fabric.

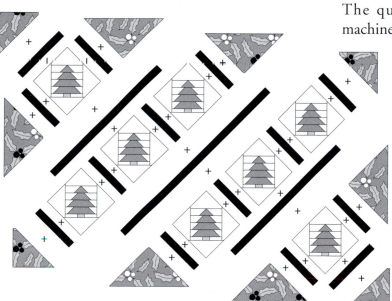

Quick Black Forest Pie

1	chocolate flavored or graham pie crust	1	package (4 serving) chocolate flavor *instant* pudding mix
8	oz. thawed whipped topping		
1	cup cold milk	1	cup cherry pie filling

Spread 1 cup of whipped topping on the bottom of the pie crust. Combine milk and pudding mix. Blend for 1 minute. Fold in 1½ cups whipped topping. Spread over whipped topping in crust. Spread remaining whipped topping over pudding. Spoon cherry pie filling in the center of the pie. Chill at least 3 hours.

Caramel Apples 🍎🍎

41" Square

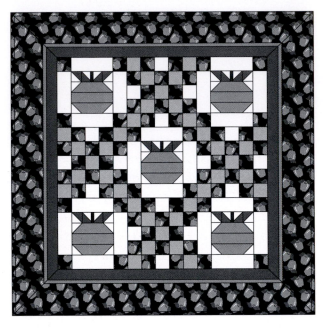

See photograph on page 45.

Living as we do in Minnesota, we certainly mark the change of the seasons. Even though it's sad to have summer ending, fall is a lovely time of the year. The apple harvest is one sure sign that summer is over and tasty treats are ahead.

Ingredients		
Fabric #1		⅓ yard red
Fabric #2		⅓ yard green
Fabric #3		¼ yard gold
Fabric #4		1⅓ yards apple print [1]
Fabric #5		⅔ yard background
Fabric #6		2" x 8" piece brown

[1] Includes double straight-of-grain binding.

This quilt combines pieced apple blocks with an old favorite pattern, Double Irish Chain. The apple print fabric in the border nicely ties together the red of the apples, green of the leaves and the caramel in the Irish Chain blocks, but you could use any print just as effectively. The apple stem is set-in using a simple technique, giving a three dimensional look.

Cutting Directions		
From	Cut	To Get
Fabric #1	3 2" strips	10 trapezoids with base cut at 6" [1]
		5 - 6½" x 2" rectangles
	4 1" strips	Middle border
Fabric #2	1 2" strip	20 Easy Angle™ triangles [2]
	4 2" strips	Inside border
Fabric #4	1 2½" strip	20 squares
	4 4½" strips	Outside border
Fabric #5	2 2" strips	20 Easy Angle™ triangles [2]
		20 Easy Angle™ orphans
	4 2½" strips	20 - 6½" x 2½" rectangles
Fabric #6	1 2" x 8"strip	5 - 1¼" x 2" rectangles

[1] The base of the trapezoid should fall on the solid line below the 6" dashed line of Companion Angle™, as if you were cutting a 6" finished size triangle (see page 10).

[2] Layer these strips right sides together and cut. They will then be ready to chain-sew into triangle squares.

Double Irish Chain Cutting	
From	Cut
Fabric #3	3 2½" strips [1]
Fabric #4	4 2½" strips [1]
Fabric #5	2 2½" strips [1]

[1] Divide each of the strips in half.

Add background triangles to all the red trapezoids. Press towards the apple.

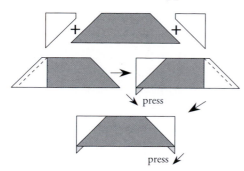

Assemble fabric #2 and #5 triangle squares. (See *Basic Ingredients*, page 15.) Press towards the green. Join these triangle squares to form leaves. You will need to make 5 pairs. Press.

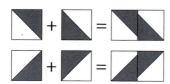

To insert the stem: fold brown rectangle in half, right sides *out*, and sew into the seam as you sew your leaf pairs together. Press this seam open on the back, having the stem opened and then centered over the seam. The stem will be "loose", which gives an interesting three dimensional look!

Assemble your apples in rows. Press.

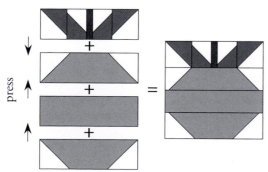

Add your background rectangles to both sides of your apple. Press. Assemble square-rectangle-square. Press. Add top and bottom strips to your apple block. Press.

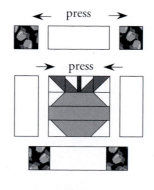

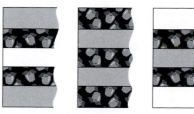

To make the Double Irish Chain blocks, make one of each of the above strip sets by sewing together the half strips that you cut from the cutting table. Press all seams one direction. Cut these sets into 2½" sections.

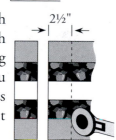

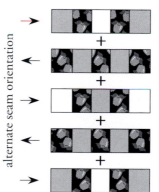

Assemble 4 blocks as diagrammed. Reverse strips as indicated to make seams alternate. Set all the blocks together, referring to the full graphic for placement.

Sew border strips together in the proper sequence. Press towards the outside edge. Add mitered borders. (See page 21.)

Diagonal lines were quilted through all the squares in the Irish Chain blocks. The apples were outlined with hand quilting, then machine meandering was done behind each apple with light thread. Parallel diagonal lines were quilted in the outside border after the inside borders were stitched in the ditch.

Use a double straight-of-grain binding in fabric #4.

Desserts

Ginger Star ❦❦

18" Square

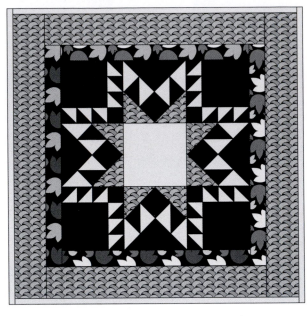

See photograph on page 45.

Ginger is just the spice to compliment the black background in this wall-hanging. Use it carefully – too much can be overpowering. Blend it with other colors and watch your star begin to truly shine.

Ingredients		
Fabric #1		⅓ yard ginger [1]
Fabric #2		⅓ yard black
Fabric #3		¼ yard green
Fabric #4		⅛ yard print

[1] Includes straight-of-grain binding.

The open areas in the center and corners give opportunities to showcase any hand-quilted design you like, making Ginger Star a lovely coffee and desert quilt.

Cutting Directions		
From	Cut	To Get
Fabric #1	1 4½" strip	1 - 4½" square
	2 1½" strips	8 Companion Angle™ triangles
		24 Easy Angle™ triangles [1]
	1 1⅞" strip	8 Easy Angle™ triangles [2]
Fabric #2	1 1½" strip	24 Easy Angle™ triangles [1]
		4 squares
	1 1⅞" strip	4 squares
		8 Easy Angle™ triangles [2]
	1 2½" strip	4 Companion Angle™ triangles
	1 3½" strip	4 squares
Fabric #3	2 2½" strips	8 Easy Angle™ orphans
		Outside border
Fabric #4	2 1½" strips	Inside border

[1] Stack strips right sides together and cut. They will then be ready to chain-sew.

[2] Stack strips right sides together and cut. They will then be ready to chain-sew. Mark your Easy Angle™ tool with masking tape 1⅞" from the black tip, or simply "eyeball" the strip edge parallel to lines on the tool.

Quilt Assembly

Stitch together the 1⅞" triangle-squares and the 1½" triangle-squares. See *Basic Ingredients*, page 15. Press towards the dark fabric.

To 4 of these triangle-squares add a 1⅞" square and fabric #1 Companion Angle™ triangle. Pay special attention to how the triangle squares are turned. Make 4 of these units.

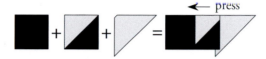

To the remaining 4 triangle-squares add a fabric #1 Companion Angle™ triangle. Press towards the triangle.

Combine these in pairs and add a fabric #2 Companion Angle™ triangle. Make 4 of these.

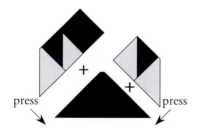

Add 2 Easy Angle™ triangles of fabric #3 to these to form 4 square blocks. Set aside.

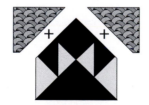

Stitch the 1½" triangle squares together into 4 each of these 2 groups:

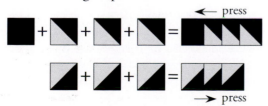

Add a 3½" square of fabric #2 to each pair of these, being careful of how these strips are turned. Make 4 of these square blocks.

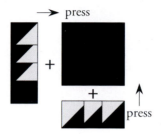

Assemble the 8 blocks you have made along with the 4½" ginger square, as indicated.

Add simple borders of fabrics #4 and #3. Quilt, bind in fabric #1, and *enjoy!*

Homemade Caramels

2	cups sugar	½	cup butter (or
1	pinch of salt		margarine)
2	cups white corn syrup	1½	cups cream (or
1	tsp. vanilla		evaporated milk)

Boil sugar, salt, and corn syrup to 245° (use a candy thermometer). Stir occasionally. Add butter and cream gradually so the mixture does not stop boiling. Cook until firm ball stage (245°), stirring occasionally. This may take 15-20 minutes. Remove from heat. Cool somewhat and pour into buttered 9" x 12" pan. Cut when cool. Wrap in squares of waxed paper.

Recipe by
Darlene Zimmerman

Oreo™ Dessert

30+	Oreo™ cookies	1	can fudge ice cream
⅓	cup butter		topping
½	gallon mint chocolate	8	oz. whipped topping
	chip ice cream		Walnuts

Crush cookies. Melt butter. Mix and press into 9" x 13" pan. Freeze 20 minutes. Spread ice cream over crust. Freeze 20 minutes. Spread fudge topping over ice cream. Freeze 20 minutes. Spread whipped topping over fudge topping. Freeze 20 minutes. Spread walnuts and more crushed cookies on top. Cover with plastic or foil and freeze. This dessert will keep in the freezer up to one month.

Recipe by
Joy Hoffman

Banana Chocolate Chip Cookies

1½	cups flour	½	cup margarine
1	tsp. baking powder	2	eggs
¼	tsp. baking soda	1	cup mashed banana
½	tsp. salt	1½	cups oatmeal
1	cup sugar	1	12 oz. pkg. mini chocolate chips

Mix together, drop on cookie sheets and bake for 12 minutes at 375°. For pan cookies, simply spread batter in a lightly greased pan and bake 15 minutes at 375° or until top springs back when gently touched.

Recipe by
Joy Hoffman

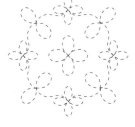

Hot Fudge Pudding Cake

1	cup flour	2	tbsp. melted shortening
¾	cup sugar	1	cup chopped nuts
2	tbsp. cocoa	1	cup brown sugar
2	tsp. baking powder	¼	cup cocoa
¼	tsp. salt	1¾	cup boiling water
½	cup milk		

Mix flour, sugar, 2 tbsp. cocoa, baking powder, and salt in a bowl. Blend in milk and melted shortening. Add nuts. Pour into an ungreased 9" x 9" pan. Stir together the brown sugar and ¼ cup cocoa. Sprinkle over batter and pour boiling water over batter. Bake 45 minutes. Turn upside down on a plate. Serve hot, preferably with ice cream.

Recipe by
Joy Hoffman

No Failure Pie Crust

3	cups flour	1	egg, well beaten
1¼	cups shortening	5	tbsp. water
1	tsp. salt	1	tbsp. vinegar

Cut shortening into salt and flour. Combine egg, water, and vinegar. Pour into flour mixture and blend with a spoon until flour is completely moistened. This is easy to handle and can be rerolled without toughening. Dough will keep in the refrigerator for up to 2 weeks. Makes 4 single crusts.

Recipe by
Joy Hoffman

Gold Rush Brownies

2	cups graham cracker crumbs	1	cup chocolate chips
1	can sweetened condensed milk	1	cup chopped walnuts (optional)

Combine all ingredients thoroughly. Spread into a 9" x 9" pan. Bake at 350° for 30-35 minutes. Mixture should pull away from the sides of the pan. Cool and cut into squares.

Recipe by
Karla Schulz

Bavarian Apple Torte

½	cup margarine	1	egg
	Sugar	4	cups peeled, sliced, and cooked apples
	Vanilla		
1	cup flour	½	tsp. cinnamon
8	oz. cream cheese	¼	cup sliced almonds

Combine margarine, ⅓ cup sugar, ¼ tsp. vanilla, and flour. Press into bottom and sides of a 10" deep-dish pie pan. Mix together well the cream cheese, ¼ cup sugar, egg, and ½ tsp. vanilla. Pour into pastry-lined pan. Toss together apples, ⅓ cup sugar, and ½ tsp. cinnamon. Spoon over cream cheese mixture. Sprinkle almonds on top. Bake at 400° for 10 minutes and 350° for 25 more minutes. Allow to cool before removing from pan.

Recipe by
Darlene Zimmerman

Quilter's Fudge

1	lb. powdered sugar	¼	cup milk
1	tsp. vanilla	½	cup cocoa
½	cup margarine (cut into pieces)	⅜	cup chopped nuts

Blend powdered sugar and cocoa in glass bowl. Add milk and margarine. *Do not mix!* Cook on high in microwave oven for 2 minutes. Stir. Add vanilla and nuts. Stir until blended. Pour into greased pan. Cool. If you desparately need chocolate fast, this dessert can be eaten hot, with a spoon.

Recipe by
Theresa Westrup

Aprons ✿✿

See photograph on page 44.

You will need ¾ yard of fabric for each apron. This pattern assumes 42"-44" wide fabric. From this piece of fabric, cut the pieces indicated at the right. Each pattern requires a pieced block for the bodice, which, by itself or with borders, measures 12½" square. Construct a single block from scraps, or you may have a favorite block left over from your latest project.

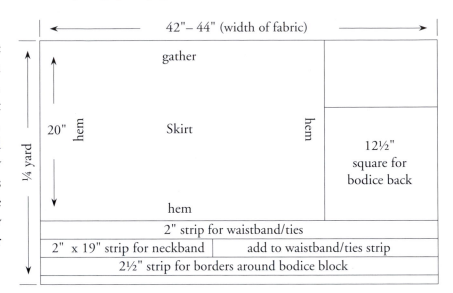

Apron Assembly

For the neckband, use the 2" x 19" strip from the apron fabric. Fold under ⅜" on both long edges and press. Fold in half so the raw edges are on the inside. Press again. Stitch ⅛" from folded edges. You can adjust the neckband to your own size.

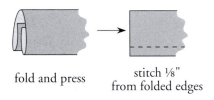

fold and press   stitch ⅛"
from folded edges

Piece your favorite block for the bodice, or follow the directions for one of our suggestions

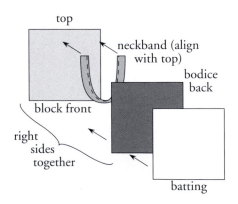

shown later. Add apron fabric borders to make the block measure 12½" square. Cut a backing piece of apron fabric 12½" square, and a piece of thin batting the same size. Layer the front and back right sides together, positioning the neck band inside, and lay the batting on top. Sew a ¼" seam on both sides and the top edge, leaving the bottom edge open for turning. Turn, bringing the neckband to the outside and press lightly. Do any quilting on the block at this time. You may also wish to top-stitch ¼" from the outside edges of the bodice.

Hem the bottom edge and sides of the skirt. Gather the top edge of the skirt ¼" from the edge.

back of skirt

Add the remainder of the neckband strip to the the 2" strip you cut for the waistband and tie to make it longer. Fold under ⅜" on both long

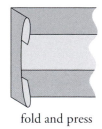

fold and press

edges and press. Also turn under and press both ends.

Center the waistband on the center of the apron bodice and topstitch ⅛" from the folded edge

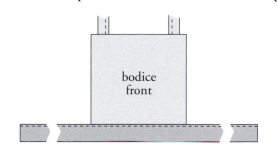

bodice front

on the waistband from end to end. (*Tip: Before sewing, try on the apron and move the waistband higher or lower on the bodice to fit you.*)

Gather the skirt, center the waistband on the skirt. (The two ends should extend beyond the skirt on both sides; these are the ties.) Again,

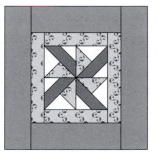

bodice front

skirt front

topstitch ⅛" from the folded edge on the waistband from end to end. Do one more line of stitching ¼" from the folded edge all the way around the waistband to hold all the raw edges in place. Now it's ready to wear!

Bodice Block Suggestions

Assemble one block according to the directions in Caramel Apples (page 82). Add inside borders of background fabric cut at 1½". Add outside borders of apron fabric cut at 2½". With your Easy

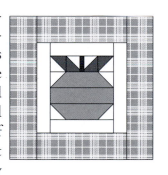

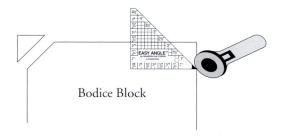

Bodice Block

Angle™, cut off the two top corners as if you were cutting a 2" triangle. Finish the apron according to the pattern directions.

Make one block according to the directions in the Mint Julep pattern (page 50). Cut 1½" borders of one of your prints for your inside border. Add outside borders cut at 2½" of the apron

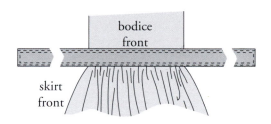

fabric. With your Easy Angle™, cut off the two top corners as if you were cutting a 2" triangle. Finish the apron according to the pattern directions.

Make one block according to the directions in the Black Forest Torte construction directions starting on page 79. However, different cutting requirements are presented here. The basic block here is slightly larger and the lower two trapezoids making up the tree are different. The basic construction method is the same as that

Garnishes

for the Black Forest Torte quilt blocks. Make the basic block with the Companion Angle™ triangle and trapezoids. Trim to 7½" square. Add inside brown border,

and outside borders cut at 2½" from apron fabric. With your Easy Angle™, cut off the two top corners as if you were cutting a 2" triangle. Finish the apron according to the pattern directions.

Use one of these blocks, or research your own quilt recipes to find a block that makes your apron special to you.

Cutting Directions - Black Forest Apron Block		
From	Cut	To Get
Green	1 2" strip	1 Companion Angle™ triangles 1 - 4" base trapezoid [1] 1 - 5" base trapezoid [1] 1 - 6" base trapezoid [1]
Background	1 2" strip	8 - 5" base trapezoids [1] 2 - 1½" x 3½" rectangles
Brown	1 1" strips 1 1½" square	Inside border Tree trunk

[1] Cut as if you were cutting Companion Angle™ triangles with this base. See page 10.

A Touch More Garnish for Good Measure

To make potholders, simply make another pieced block and border it with your same apron fabric, making it any size you wish. You can use the apron fabric for the back or just use muslin. Use *cotton* batting inside the potholder, as polyester melts when heated. Baste your three layers together, quilt and bind as you would any quilt. Use and enjoy!

Bon Appetit and Happy Quilting

Notes

Notes